If Sally's triumph is as contagious as her joy, everyone will win by reading her inspirational story. Knowing Sally is pure delight—there never was a cloud the sun couldn't shine through! Every setback has a silver lining—and any challenge that Sally has been given is transformed to inspiration. She is proof that the human spirit rises!

—*Amy Freeze, WABC-TV meteorologist,*
five-time Emmy winner; mother of four,
nine-time marathoner, fan of the underdog

If you would have told me that the girl I met in kindergarten would end up being such a huge inspiration in my adult life, I wouldn't have believed you. Sally's challenges and how she's chosen to deal with and overcome them are equally as moving as her drive to help others with their lives. I'm thrilled she's getting her message out to the world!

—*Van Romaine, producer, composer, musician*

To say that Sally Kalksma is the living embodiment of resilience, both physically as well as psychologically, would be an enormous understatement. Hit with numerous challenges that would have stopped most people in their tracks, Sally stood strong and faced her obstacles head on, not only surviving but thriving—including becoming one of the top-ranked stair-climbing racers in the world. Sally's passion for life is truly infectious—prepare to be inspired by her incredible resilience, lust for life, and true grit. Everyone who comes into contact with Sally walks away a better person, and I feel extremely fortunate to call her a friend.

—*Tom Holland, exercise physiologist, bestselling author,*
elite endurance athlete, fitness personality

To already have a magnetic, bubbly spirit, and then conquer adversity and live life more fully than before, that's inspiration—that's Sally. She is a firecracker . . . she already had an energetic spark for life, and now she is a grand finale that leaves you in greater awe and inspired by what's possible.

—*Dianne DeOliveira, award-winning journalist, on-air personality, world-ranked masters runner, and owner of Bella N Motion, a USATF running club for women*

LIFE GETS IN THE WAY

Powering Through Adversity with Grit and Grace

Sally Kalksma

HybridGlobal
PUBLISHING

Published by
Hybrid Global Publishing
301 East 57th Street
4th Floor
New York, NY 10022

Printed in the United States of America, or in the United Kingdom when distributed elsewhere.

Kalksma, Sally
Life Gets in The Way: Powering Through Adversity with Grit and Grace
    ISBN: 978-1-951943-29-5
    eBook: 978-1-951943-30-1
    LCCN: 2020914941

Cover design by: Natasha Clawson
Copyediting and interior design by: Claudia Volkman
Author photo by: Tom Zapcic Photography

www.sallykalksma.com

DEDICATION

This book is dedicated to my children: Paula, Sam, and Dana. They have grown into the kind of adults I strive to be.

CONTENTS

FOREWORD

When I met Sally Kalksma, just over ten years ago, it was one of those rare moments where your dull, black-and-white world turns Technicolor.

Ironically, though we had not met yet, we were living very similar and parallel lives: We both grew up not too far from one another in northern New Jersey. We both ran track in high school and in fact, unbeknownst to us, had competed in the same meets. After college, we both worked and played in New York City (Sally definitely had more fun than me!) before marrying the loves of our lives and moving to the burbs. We both went on to have three children, boy–girl twins and a single birth. Sally's newborn was even treated at the same hospital where I had been born. Sally and I were both stay-at-home moms who, later on as adults, found our way back to our love of running.

Sally followed her passion for running by becoming the race director for a popular local race, the Pine Beach 5K. I, on the other hand, found myself working part-time at a running magazine, *Running Times*, to connect my love for running to my return to the workplace. Later on, after I met Sally, I realized that I had processed her race ads in the magazine for many years!

Then in 2011, multiple myeloma, a deadly blood cancer that is still considered to be incurable, brought us together.

By this time, I had found a way to take my knowledge of the running industry, honed at *Running Times*, to start a national fundraising "Endurance Program" at a highly regarded cancer nonprofit, the Multiple Myeloma Research Foundation (MMRF), which was located in the town next to mine. I didn't know the first thing about cancer when I joined the foundation, and I could hardly spell the words *multiple myeloma*. But I learned quickly that multiple myeloma is a blood cancer that develops in the bone marrow, the soft spongy tissue found in the bone's center. As in all cancers, the diseased cells grow out of control. In myeloma, this results in the crowding out of the healthy blood cells, leading to bone damage that causes bone pain and lesions, weakening the bones and making fractures commonplace. Patients can suffer from anemia, excessive bleeding, and a compromised immune system, making them more susceptible to infection. The buildup of protein in the blood and urine can damage the kidneys and other organs. In a word, myeloma is terrible.

Our Endurance Program began in 2008 as a way to raise vital funds to fuel life-saving research for the MMRF. We'd enlist runners to fundraise via world-class marathons like Boston and New York City. But things took off fast, and we soon expanded our program to include other types of running events, including the Empire State Building Run-Up, the most prestigious "tower race" in the world. We learned quickly that a whole bunch of people were crazy enough to want to take on this "vertical marathon" (1,576 steps/86 floors) up the famed Empire State Building. In fact, these fanatic runners were so passionate about running from the lobby of the ESB to the Observation Deck a quarter mile up above Fifth Avenue that they would raise an average of eight thousand dollars each if they were selected for the team.

The same year that I started with the MMRF, Sally heard the words that no one ever wants to hear: "You've got cancer." Sally, always finding her own unique way through adversity, discovered stair climbing as a way to cope with her myeloma diagnosis and the recent death of her husband from another type of cancer. She would put all of her sorrow, frustration, fear, and energy into running stairs—at lunch, after work, and on weekends. "Tower Running" became her passion. So, in 2011, when she learned the MMRF was to be the exclusive charity partner for the Empire State Building, she was all in. And that is when we finally met.

Sally had a gift for running up tall buildings, and she used that to raise tens of thousands of dollars for the breakthrough research being conducted by the MMRF. She quickly rose to become an elite climber on the "Tower Running" circuit, earning an international ranking and being invited to run such prestigious races as the Eiffel Tower. Her enthusiasm for stair climbing, for raising research funds, and indeed for life was contagious, so she became a "media darling" for the MMRF, garnering a lot of attention to raise awareness and hope for myeloma patients.

I'm excited and honored to write this foreword because I know that you will read it and get the essence of what I have received from my friendship with Sally: You will meet a woman who lifts you up and brightens your outlook on simply everything. You will meet effervescence personified. You will meet a woman who has lived through trauma, heartbreak, and suffering, the likes of which would break any ordinary human being. You will see someone who has stared death in the face and shouted—with the biggest smile on her face and a glint in her eye: "Cancer, you picked the WRONG woman!"

Working with cancer patients exposes me to witness a lot of pain and suffering, but it has also afforded me the privilege of getting to know some of the most incredibly strong and inspiring souls on the planet. I put Sally at the top of that list.

I know you will enjoy her story and come away inspired. She will teach you to find joy, gather your grit in difficult times, and shine even in the most difficult of moments.

—*Jane Hoffman,* Associate Director, Team for Cures,
Multiple Myeloma Research Foundation

INTRODUCTION

I should have been dead. Don't get me wrong—I do not have a death wish. I love life, even though my quest for adventure has put me in some life-threatening situations. Some of my antics were youth-based stupidity—like the time I was dragged on roller skates by a car going 50 mph, or the time I ripped open the veins in my legs hopping a chain-link fence running from the police. I've also done more than my fair share of illegal and legal drugs (the prescription stuff, thanks to my current health status). I'll blame peer pressure on the illegal stuff—more on that later. However, if I could have traded places with loved ones who have suffered and those who have died, I would have. But I wasn't given that choice. (Spoiler alert for those who don't want to read the whole book: I survived!)

Those of you who are planning to read the entire book will be happy you did—you may just get inspired to live life like it's the last day earth will be in existence. (And I don't mean like it's your last day and you're lying in a hospital bed. I mean like it's Armageddon—the end of the world.) I hope to inspire you to stop wasting time worrying but instead use every minute possible to enjoy life—because you're never going to get the chance again to live this very moment. I want to empower you to do what you always dreamed of doing. Let nothing, let nobody, stand in your way. Do not wait until life throws you a curve ball to make the change because that just might be your third strike.

Speaking of lying in a hospital bed, did you catch the part where I said I survived—past tense? I had cancer. Let me repeat, I *HAD* cancer. Did you also get my reference to choosing death? It's true. I would have let cancer beat me if it meant that others could have won. That was the one time in my life I would have preferred to lose, but no, that didn't happen. Therefore, I had to make the best of the situation.

My late husband and best friend, Pete, passed away in 2009 from a very brief, eight-month battle with melanoma caused by a genetic disorder. A year prior to his death, I was diagnosed with multiple myeloma. Soon after his death, I found out that two of my three children possessed the same genetic disorder as their father. I took my negative feelings out on the stairs—yes, you read the right . . . the stairs. I ran up the stairs as fast as I could to relieve the stress. Eventually this stress reliever put me in the best shape of my life and got me a world ranking . . . in stair climbing. Yes, it's actually a sport.

I am now a professional stair climber, a motivational speaker, a writer, and a video talk show host, none of which I planned to be. These accomplishments are all the results of life getting in the way. I hope my story can empower you to go for your dreams, because *Life Gets in the Way* is not just my story—it's anyone's story who thinks they can't handle life's challenges. I wish I could tell you that this is a book about overcoming adversity, but unfortunately, it's not. Nor is it a "tell all" book. Along the way, I'll name some names, but others I will keep a secret—and that is not to protect the innocent, but rather not give the guilty any extra attention they DO NOT deserve. (Yeah, you know who you are.) This book is about fighting through adversity. It's about grit. I found inspiration in obstacles, and joy in overcoming them. You can too!

1

GENESIS

June 12, 1967
Dear Diary,
Today I ran to the beach with Marion. I didn't stop once!
Mom said I ran a mile. I can't wait to go again. It was fun.
Love, Sally

Whoever came up with the theory that the eldest child in the family is the smartest while the youngest seeks rebellion by attention must have studied my family. It's really funny that they seldom mention anything about the middle child, especially if there is more than one. And in my family, there are three.

Being the youngest caused me to seek a lot of attention, aka rebellion. Luckily, to save me from being a total derelict, my four older siblings were great role models. I wanted to be just like my big sisters. I did everything they did—which was good and bad since they were a lot older than me. I grew up fast. And what I lacked in brains I got in street smarts, which I believe is a higher form of intelligence that can take you just as far if not farther than a 4.0 GPA. I would never have told my three children this while they were growing up, but since they were all student athletes who have achieved post-graduate educations,

I can say this now. You know, the old "do what I say, not what I do" way of parenting.

September 1, 1969
Dear Diary,
I won the 50-yard dash and the pie-eating contest at Field Day. I like blueberry the best. I got two blue ribbons.
Sally

When I was younger, I wanted to be a lawyer and write a book. Well, since I lacked that smart gene, I choose the latter, and at the age of fifty-five, I've shed my inhibitions and started to share what I wrote. Age has never stopped me from doing what I wanted. When I was too young, I did it anyway. When people tell me I'm too old to do something, I still do it. Why would I let anybody or anything, especially a number, stop me? I love to challenge myself. People say I'm competitive, and maybe I am. But I'm most competitive with myself. I always want to better myself. And when I feel I have mastered something, I look for something new. Some people also confuse conceit with self-confidence. I'm not self-centered; I just have a high self-esteem.

I learned two important lessons at a young age; the first was to train my brain. If you say you won't or you can't, your brain will send receptors out to the rest of your body, and it will not do it. I trained my brain with lots of repetition, just like anything you want to master. I just kept telling myself over and over that I could do something until my body did what my brain told it to do. I trained my brain like I trained my muscles. The workout was to be positive—to only emit positive thoughts so my brain could only send positive receptors out to the rest of my body. Like any workout, I had good and bad days. Sometimes it didn't work, but I would try harder the next time.

I started to train my brain at a young age when I started running. I wanted to run because all my sisters ran. I told myself if they could do it, then I could too. Instinctively I trained my brain to be positive physically as well as mentally. Being positive now comes naturally.

I decided that I would only think and speak positively. Think of it like using the present tense and the past tense. Present tense is positive. Past tense is negative. I never use negative words when I'm trying to accomplish anything. When running a race, I do not say, "I am NOT going to let her win." Instead I say, "I AM going to win." By using the positive present tense in everything I do, being positive now comes naturally. Try it—you'll see that it works.

RUNNING DIARY
DATE: May 3, 1975
EVENT: Junior Olympic One Mile Run
COMMENTS: 2nd place; I couldn't catch Joetta Clark.
Don't give up. Do it now!

This mindset gave me the ability to excel in running at a young age. But I also had to learn how to lose. No one is ever going to be on top forever. When I was twelve, I learned how to lose gracefully when I came up against my biggest competitor to date. I'll never forget that day. I checked into the paddock before the one-mile run at the Junior Olympic Championship and saw a tall, lean girl walking very confidently. She had spikes thrown over her muscular shoulder. No one my age had muscles defined like that, let alone wore spikes. I was instantly psyched out. I didn't know it then, but this was someone I would have to run against and lose to in every big meet for the next six years. Being second to three-time Olympian Joetta Clark taught me to be humble, something I sorely needed. She and her father, the famed high school principal Joe Clark, featured in the true 1989 movie *Lean on Me*, inspired me.

The running boom of the seventies had just begun, and I was part of it. Although the women's movement helped Title 9 in college, youth sports and high schools didn't quite recognize girls' running as much. My father decided I needed a coach, so he contacted a former student of his, marathon great Tom Fleming. My mother had to drive me all over New Jersey and New York to compete. My sisters Pat and Sue started the girls' cross country team their senior year in high school. When I entered the following year, there were not enough girls in the sport, so I had to compete on the boys' JV team. I earned the number-one spot. That spring I was only allowed to run the one mile in track, as anything more was considered too taxing on the female body. As a freshman in high school, I made it to the Meet of Champions.

Running gave me the attention the youngest child craves. But remember, along with that attention comes rebellion. I swear (and I don't swear), if I were in high school now and did just one of the things I did when I was younger, I probably would be in juvie. Thank God (and I'm not religious either), it was the seventies and you could get away with a lot as long as your parents didn't find out. It's not a coincidence that I'm sharing some of these stories now that my parents are deceased.

Our generation was probably more afraid of our parents than the police. At one point my parents threatened to pull me out of Glen Ridge High School, located in the beautiful upper-class small town located just fifteen miles west of New York City, and send me to Point Pleasant Boro High School, in the Jersey shore town where my parents owned a summer home. You would never think that I was born in Newark, New Jersey, and spent the first four years of my life in East Orange, New Jersey, until my father had the foresight to move his family out of there before the race riots hit in the 1960s.

For many growing up is not easy, and I was no exception. Not only was I in the shadow of my four talented sisters, but I was also the daughter of a great football player and coach. My dad was a man who played in the era of leather helmets and coached at a time when an adult had the authority to discipline and was respected for it. My dad was inducted into the New Jersey High School Coaches' Hall of Fame alongside Vince Lombardi.

I can thank my mother, who modeled in her twenties, for my legs, but I thank my father for giving me the grit to use them. That grit gets me through every obstacle I encounter, whether I have chosen that hurdle or it is thrown out before me. Grit is the power to turn the switch in your brain so it puts your body into another gear. Grit is what makes you tough. I trained my brain to be tough. That gave me grit. You can use grit in sports, and you can use grit in any adverse situation you need to get through. In high school I used this grit to run races, as well as to run from the police once or twice. Now I channel this grit into tower running, facing health issues, and dealing with tough mental situations.

When you use grit enough times, it becomes an instinct. At the age of ten, grit got me to pedal my bike home a mile away with the bottom of my foot slit wide open and bleeding from the base of my toes to the heel. A year later I instinctively used grit to save my life when I fell off the end of the jetty into the Atlantic Ocean. I just clawed my way back up the slippery

algae with the rough waves slamming my body between the rocks. I didn't say to myself, "It's time to use grit." I just made it happen. When your brain is trained, you can turn the switch in your head and your body will obey. Grit took over after I was hit by a car. I am not saying grit gave me super-human powers to deflect the vehicle making an illegal turn, but it did give me the power to not let this setback destroy my spirit to get better and eventually return stronger than before.

I think I had the same look on my face whether I was running a race or running from the police back in high school.

I have to thank my father for not raising any "daddy's little girls." In fact, I was an accident, and I was also my parent's last hope for a boy. I was even named after my father, Salvatore. No, my real name is not Salvatore, but Sally is the closest feminine version to it. It's no wonder my biggest fantasy was not to be a prima ballerina, but to be a kicker in the NFL. Maybe that's in part due to the fact I wasn't one of the daughters given dance lessons.

RUNNING DIARY
DATE: May 20, 1978
EVENT: State Finals
RACE: One Mile 5:25
COMMENTS: pb, school record, 4th place. I was disqualified for cutting in too early. I hate running!

The second lesson I learned at a young age is that only I have the power to change myself and my circumstances. I found this out the hard way when I kissed a boy, and he not only told everyone but exaggerated the story and gave me a reputation I did not deserve. From that moment on I knew I had to be with good people if I wanted good things to happen. To this day I stay clear of toxic individuals. Life is too short and valuable to be disrespected and depreciated. Never listen to passive-aggressive people who put others down to make themselves feel better. Stay away from negative people and those who talk bad about others, as it is a sign of their weakness and insecurity. But do not be too quick to find fault with others, as it does not make you appear smarter, only sinister.

Not everyone has to go on to college to become successful. You just need to become a productive part of society, not a problem. In fact, the most accomplished classmate of mine decided to pursue his dreams instead of furthering his education. Tommy Mapother—or as I nicknamed him, The Kentucky Kisser (I really don't think I need to explain much more than that he had moved from the Bluegrass State to our town)—went on to become Tom Cruise. He was good-looking, athletic, talented, and most importantly, a nice person. He said he wanted to be an actor, and he did it. I have no doubt he has grit. He did not listen to other people who doubted he could succeed in such a competitive field, something that I regret. (No, I didn't want to be an actress.)

I didn't want to go to college either. I wanted to join the army, but I didn't have a choice. I had to listen to my father for once. My father, the son of Sicilian immigrants, was the first in his family to go to college, thanks to a full football scholarship. He made sure his five daughters all went to college. He also wanted to see all five of his daughters get married. He was able to witness four weddings before his death. Can you guess who he didn't walk down the aisle? Anyway, I begrudgingly went off to Glassboro State College, while many of my friends from our upper-class hometown went off to schools like MIT, Boston University, and Wellesley. My high school boyfriend even attended West Point Military Academy. Not serving my country is one of my biggest regrets.

Not only did I not want to attend school, I no longer wanted to run. I gave up on the authority figures I thought were supposed to mentor me. The teachers and coaches I had in high school did not fight for me, and I felt they kicked me when I was down. Therefore, I did not fight for them when I got on the line to run a race. By my junior year in high school, I no longer tried. I could still win, but I didn't care to. Why should I kill myself for someone who didn't fight for me when I was disqualified in the State Finals track meet? Why should I kill myself for someone who didn't help me when the authorities found Jack Daniels and rolling paraphernalia in my possession as a setup? I lost any chance of a track scholarship, and they didn't try to help me. Rebellion at its finest set in. Again, I knew only I could make my life better. I felt it was me versus the world.

RUNNING LOG
DATE: July 28, 1980
EVENT: Lakewood Roller Rink
RACE: First speed skating practice
COMMENTS: More like roller derby, not sure about this

In college, I found it wasn't just me against the world. It was me fighting the world, and I suddenly realized I no longer had to. I let go of the built-up anger I had inside. Once I did that, I was immediately happier. I started to enjoy running again. I was coerced into joining the cross country and track team by a coach, Nancy Buhrer, who believed in me (and therefore I believed in her), and I ran well. Like anyone who works hard, I was rewarded; my reward was being named captain of both sports my junior and senior years.

Don't let this fairy tale fool you, though. I still had my appetite for fun. When I wasn't running, I was out having a good time and causing mischief. I excelled in my classes, too—partly because my parents said I had to pay for half of my education, and partly because I took classes I was interested in. My senior year was a far cry from my first week as a freshman when I was almost thrown out of school for "accidentally" trespassing in a factory one night trying to find my way back to my dorm from a party that was broken up by the police. I learned a lot in college, and it wasn't all in a classroom. I got higher education courses in street smarts.

During this time, I forged friendships with three woman who would turn out to be my closest friends for life. Pam (Okilita) Caucino, SueAnn (Glester) Carurso, and Linda Schlachter are the type of friends that are there no matter what, like family. We all need friends like that, both male and female. Women take note: never lose your girlfriends! A man isn't going to tell you to put baby powder in your pumps when the sides rub against your feet too much. Only a woman can give you tips like that. You know what a man will say? "Buy more comfortable shoes." And men, here's some advice for you, too: don't ever lose your male friends either, because most women don't want to talk about car chassis unless you're repairing it for them. True friendships are invaluable. Like all types of good relationships, they must be nourished so they can flourish. Give them attention and love, yet space to grow on their own. If you neglect or abuse them, they will go away.

Another thing happened in college: I met someone who would constantly change my life for the next thirty-plus years and test my will. Testing my will was not a challenge I was prepared for at the age of eighteen, but with time and repetition I learned to adapt and persevere. Little did I know that spring day of my freshman year when I was working out in the college weight room that Pete was overcoming the removal of a neurogenic tumor on his lung. Nor did I know he would end up being my husband.

I met Pete during the fall of my freshman year at Glassboro State when I roller-skated past his apartment. However, we didn't "hook up" until we reconnected months later after talking in the weight room. This was less than a month after he had surgery—surgery, he nonchalantly mentioned, to remove his right sixth rib because of a tumor grow-

Pete and I were always there for each other in time of need. Here he is carrying me when I broke my foot in college.

ing on his lung. This rare neurilemoma was a nerve tumor that turns malignant. On one of our first dates he showed me his rib, and I mean he actually handed it to me. Eventually he gave me his rib as a souvenir. This was a better love story than Adam and Eve. How could I not fall in love? I loved his sense of humor. His determination to get back in shape was amazing. His work ethic was phenomenal. His drive was admirable. Probably because he had had lots of experience—this was not his first tumor. Pete had grit. Together we were not going to sit down and look for four leaf clovers. We were going to grow them.

2

IN SICKNESS AND IN HEALTH

RUNNING LOG
DATE: 4/18/84
DISTANCE: 1,500 meters
TIME: 5:01
NOTES: Last home college track meet. Felt great.

When I say, "This wasn't supposed to be my life. I'm supposed to be on Rodeo Drive," I'm not joking.

After graduating with a BA in communications, I landed an entry-level job at a recording studio on 42nd Street in New York City. Other than recording one of Billy Joel's albums, the studio primarily recorded jingles for commercials. I needed more. Not that I was ready for the big time at the age of twenty-one, but I wanted to do more than answer phones and work for "free." Mark Freeh owned Uptown Chelsea Sound, also known as Chelsea Studios, and I barely made enough money for my weekly bus pass in and out of the tunnel. (The saying in the recording industry was "When you worked for Mark, you worked for Freeh.") Thank God I didn't have to pay rent—and thank God I didn't have to live with my parents. At this time, my parents were living at our home "down the shore" while making renovations so they could live there year round.

Once again, I hate to admit, my father was right; I needed a real job and one with benefits. He was an old-fashioned man who wanted to make sure all five of his daughters could support themselves. He worked harder than his immigrant father had, holding three jobs so his family could live in an upper middle-class town and enjoy a second home at the beach.

By this time Pete was unhappy with his job too. He decided to take a huge chance, leave his safe managerial job at the quarry, take all the money he had saved up, and attend commercial dive school in southern California. I backed his decision, and we both agreed to try to have a nonexclusive long-distance relationship. Yeah, you can just imagine how that turned out—he in LA, and me in NYC . . . during the eighties.

After seven months at Chelsea Sound, I quit my job, with no future and no plans. I hit the pavement, delivering my résumé all over the tri-state area until a safe job offer came along from MGM/United Artists. My title may have sounded glamorous for a twenty-two-year-old, but the job was anything but. I partied with more celebrities at Chelsea, thanks to invites from assistant engineers and producers' assistants who needed a young attractive woman on their arm so they looked as if they were as successful as their bosses. I actually liked that job. What was there not to like about a backstage pass to Bruce Springsteen, where John Entwistel from The Who tells you that you have nice legs? (How's that for name-dropping!)

My eight months employed as an administrative assistant to the producer to the auxiliary rights at MGM/UA was one of the best learning experiences of my life. In this position, I not only saw how professional the corporate world was, I also saw how dirty the entertainment industry could be, thanks to my boss' attraction to his "glorified secretary." I took that experience straight to my interview at Atlantic Records. They came across the résumé I had dropped off earlier that year, and I jumped at the offer to be the traffic manager at their recording studio on Columbus Circle. I was on my way to having a career, and I was working at my dream job.

My corner office was enormous, with floor-to-ceiling windows overlooking the southwest end of Central Park. When my boss was strung out on heroin, the assistant studio manager would come into my office, turn the music up, put one leg on my desk and play air guitar while he prepped me on the upcoming sessions. The assistant studio manager's top desk drawer had more drugs and alcohol than office supplies. Most everyone employed by the studio thought I was a narc. They couldn't understand why I would rather go running after work than party. One of them once said, "You have a good body—why do you want to run?"

I told my children I want this picture of me used at my "celebration of life" party when I die. They are not to have a funeral—I want a party with an open bar and hors d'oeuvres.

RUNNING LOG
DATE: 8/8/86
DISTANCE: Designated Runner
TIME: Softball game
NOTES: Atlantic Studios vs Atlantic Records. Fun time: Little Steven was on our team. I helped him shop for sneakers before the game. He got black hi-tops.

I carefully picked the events I attended. I didn't want to become one of those burnt-out thirty-year-old women I saw at every party. Although they were less than ten years my senior, the lines on their faces told the story of years of partying, sleeping with the band, and still looking for love. I promised myself I wouldn't be doing this job when I was in my thirties. I occasionally did a line or took a hit so my co-workers knew I was cool with it. And besides, I did enjoy it.

There is one day I will never forget, nor do I want to. It was the beginning of my fairy-tale life—the life I thought I should lead, the road I started to take, but then turned back, like a compass pointing me in the direction I should go instead of the direction I wanted to go.

"That day" the studio manager and his assistant informed me that two extremely important young producers would be coming into the studio to set up their upcoming recording sessions. I was instructed to give them anything they wanted. What I didn't know was that it would mean my heart.

Joe was your quintessential artist. He studied at Julliard but kept an edgy look with his dirty blond mullet, trendy tee, and skin-tight designer jeans that were two sizes too small. Despite the fact that I did not find this look attractive, his personality was. I could tell he was happy to work with me on his upcoming recording project. He was a complete gentleman, well-educated and well-spoken. I later found out he was the son of the great Arif Mardin, co-founder of Atlantic Records and producer to Aretha Franklin, Bette Midler, the Bee Gees, Chaka Khan, to name just a few.

Later that day, a grin entered my office. His smile walked through the door along with his "real" torn jeans on his tall, medium build. I couldn't help but think, *This guy is supposed to be important?* as I looked at his wrinkled button-down shirt that was not meant to be unbuttoned as low as it was. He sported a baseball hat with wiry, unkempt black hair falling out from under to his open collar. He never took his eyes off me, and he never took the smile off his face nor the hat off his head, as he pulled the chair closer to my desk and sat diagonally across from me. I couldn't help myself from smiling at all the energy he brought into the room. And I couldn't help saying the first thing that came to my mind: "So I don't know who you are, but I'm told you are really important, so I'm supposed to give you anything you want." His smile got bigger, and Mark Ross, the son of Steven Ross, president and CEO of Time/Warner, once again got what he wanted, just like he had his entire privileged life.

After Pete graduated from dive school, he returned from California and we picked up where we left off. He started his career as a commercial diver. When we went out together, people didn't know who to engage a conversation with: the professional diver who salvaged ships, bridges, and planes all over the world; or me, who could tell them what I really thought of Mick Jagger when I finally met my teen crush, or the time I sat next to Quincey Jones on the private Warner Brothers' jet.

After one year, though, my dream job was in jeopardy because the in-house studio was becoming a thing of the past and could no longer compete with independent studios such as the Hit Factory. Although Atlantic Studios was available to any artist with any label, the upper management at The Rock, aka the corporate offices at Rockefeller Center, found it to be a liability. Maybe the fact that the studio was also dealing drugs had something to do with it. The receptionist was so stoned, he slurred his words on the phone—not quite an ideal attribute for that particular job. However, he did an outstanding job monitoring all the security cameras in and around the building for a bust. It really was a fun place to work, but then I was offered an even better job in the A&R (artist & repertoire) department. I could have the chance to mold an artist! However, timing is everything, and I didn't have the time. Another job was calling me—an offer of obligation.

Pete had been diagnosed with a schwannoma, a nerve sheath tumor, on his left leg. Schwannomas are usually benign, but in rare cases they can be malignant. Pete had this malignancy, also called a soft tissue sarcoma. One year later he had a neurogenic malignant sarcoma removed from the same leg. Instead of growing on the nerves, this rare cancer grows on bones and tissues. The doctors at Mt. Sinai Hospital in New York City had to remove his entire tibia. They told him he would never run again. I said goodbye to my job, to New York City, and to Mark—the first of many goodbyes over the next several years. At least I wasn't going to be another burnt-out thirty-year-old groupie working in the music business.

I did not sacrifice my dreams for Pete's dreams. I sacrificed my dreams for *him*, and I made new ones. This is what we all must learn to do if we want to be happy and not hold on to the past. "Go with the flow" does not mean being a sheep and following others blindly; it means adjusting to life, not holding on to regrets, anger, and "what-ifs." This was the fork in the road. At the time, it didn't even seem to be a decision or a choice. I was drawn to help Pete, period. The magnet of the compass led me down this road.

I gave Pete what little money I had saved, and we bought a small, three-bedroom ranch on an acre of land in South Jersey. It was the perfect place for him—an ideal location midway between Atlantic City and Philadelphia, two places he was getting a lot of dive work prior to his surgery. He had no doubt that he would run again, let alone go back to the lucrative dive career he made for himself.

While Pete recouped from having an entire bone removed from his leg, I immersed myself in my new job as Pete's full-time patient advocate and caretaker. Some of my duties included helping him walk, scheduling all his tests and doctors' appointments, and arguing with insurance companies, the latter of which I am now an expert. Other than being a mother, this job has been my most important, most fulfilling, and most difficult. It tested my mental toughness, and like anything I do, I wanted to master it and do my best. As the saying goes, "practice make perfect"—and I had a lot of practice, as Pete had another schwannoma removed from his left ankle.

Once Pete was back on his feet (no pun intended), I hit the pavement again, only this time in Philadelphia. I contemplated working at a new recording studio located in West Philly but opted for something closer to home. I landed a job at the Audio-Visual Center in Center City, Philadelphia, managing their location at the Cherry Hill Inn in Cherry Hill, New Jersey. My office was housed in the basement of this grand hotel and conference center built in 1954. The beautiful mahogany lobby was a stark contrast to the asbestos-lined hallways used for employees only. I still wonder to this day why the hotel abruptly shut their door one night, why they had a problem with the permits when it came to the demolishment, and why several co-workers have since died from cancer.

During this time life went on, including my father's demise from a misdiagnosed concussion. Several years earlier he had broken up a fight at the high school where he was employed. After getting punched, he complained to the doctors about all the pain he was having throughout his body. The diagnosis was a concussion from the hit. It was too late for him by the time they figured out it was cancer. I watched this disease take a strong man and crumble him. It was unfathomable.

RUNNING LOG
DATE: JUNE 5, 1988
DISTANCE: 6 Miles
TIME: 43:52
NOTES: Ran hard to boardwalk and fartleked (see appendix) on the way back—thinking about yesterday:

Daddy's dying and it's not a pretty sight
Daddy's dying but he's giving it a good fight
I came home and surprised my parents tonight
I came home and things didn't feel right
I couldn't get my key in the door
I heard my dad's walker cross the kitchen floor
I kissed him hello and gave him a box of chocolates from the candy store
I felt out of place as we watched TV
I showed him pictures of Pete, the dog, and me
My dad moaned, took his medication, and went to bed
My mom sat in her chair, alcohol and depression running through her head
I decided to go visit my sister Sue, but she was out of town
I thought I'd call Pat, but my mom said she wasn't around

On this particular day, I experienced another regret. Although it seems small, years earlier my dad extended an olive branch to me after all my rebellious years by inviting me to dinner, but I opted to work out instead. This regret taught me an invaluable lesson that has led me to compartmentalize my life.

I make a large mental square. That square represents my life. I draw smaller boxes within the square; these smaller boxes represent family, friends, training, racing, my job, home, and "other." Some of the boxes are larger than others. The size represents the time and energy I allot for each. Each box may change its size depending on what is happening and is most important in my life at that time. However, all the boxes must fit in the larger square. So, if I want to work out more, I must give up a little someplace else. This helps me concentrate on what is most important in my life at the time, yet still do everything I want.

When I spend time on that one square, I make sure I devote everything I have to that particular activity in order to get the best result. The only exception is when I go on a long run. I love to let my mind do whatever it wants at that time, be it plan, write, contemplate, or dream. Within the squares, I can make smaller squares. For example, in my "home" square, I can choose to give certain things more or less time and energy, like cleaning. I encourage you to try this if you feel

overwhelmed with everything in your life. I know what you're thinking: "Why don't you just make a pie chart?" I'm not sure of the answer,
but I think it might be because my square resembles a Rubik's Cube,
something I'm always trying to master and can't!

My entire life I've shared my birthday with Father's Day, whether
June 19 landed on that Sunday or not. In 1988 my twenty-sixth birthday actually landed on Father's Day, so Pete decided to kill two birds
with one stone—a diamond stone. We took a trip to see my parents,
and Pete asked my father for permission to marry me. My father wanted us to get married right away, but I wanted to plan a humungous
party, which I did. He passed away two-and-a-half months later, never
getting his Sicilian wish to see all five of his daughters married.

I have learned to forgive myself for not fulfilling my dad's dream.
You cannot fulfill other people's dreams. I love to please people—I
think this comes from my childhood when I idolized Barbara Eden in
I Dream of Jeannie. It gives me great pleasure to see other people happy,
but I wanted to be happy on my most important day. There is no fault
in pleasing yourself, sometimes at the expense of others. I'm not saying
to intentionally hurt anyone; just don't hurt yourself while trying to
make others happy. You have to let go of guilt; you have to forgive
yourself and your regrets if you want to be happy. Let go. Don't forget
the past; just don't beat yourself up about it. Why self-inflict your own
wounds? Use your past as your own private, customized tutor for a
positive learning experience. And if you think you don't have anything
to learn from your past, then look at someone else's. Try to take away
something from every situation you're in, and every person you meet,
bad or good.

3

DR. KALKSMA

JOURNAL
DATE: August 26, 1990: One-year wedding anniversary!
WEEK 32: Up 18 lbs.
NOTES: Ran/walked two miles along power line trail with Pete. Baby is causing cramps.

Life was good again. Pete was healthy. Our definition of healthy would probably alarm most people—just a few small tumors every year or so. I used to tease Pete and tell him his body was like the game Operation. As long as his nose didn't light up red, we were good. This childhood board game tested your dexterity by trying to remove body parts with an itsy-bitsy pair of tweezers. If you touched the wrong body part, the patient's nose lit up red and you lost. Our mutual sense of humor was a great coping skill. However, when it came to our children's health, we didn't joke around.

Our first baby was born four weeks premature. Nothing to be alarmed about, especially since I didn't even know I was giving birth. Yes, I knew I was pregnant, but no, I didn't think I was about to give birth when I drove myself to the hospital with bad stomach cramps in the middle of the night. Unfortunately, Pete was out of town on a dive job and did not witness the birth of his healthy, beautiful six-pound daughter, Paula, on September 21st.

After the birth of our first child, Pete and I decided to move to Pine Beach, a small Jersey shore town, closer to family and to civilization. I remember telling Pete that I didn't want any more children until he got a clean bill of health. At this point the doctors were not concerned about a genetic mutation. Therefore, according to the doctors, if he didn't have a tumor, he was fine.

That is, until Pete's maternal cousin died in March 1992, during my second pregnancy. His illness and eventual death were kept secret. Nobody outside of his immediate family was quite sure what Gary died of. Eventually we were told melanoma. We thought it was a cover. Then we all surmised that since he was a wealthy playboy who was so well-tanned from constant vacations, perhaps all that sun really did do the final damage. In the mid-eighties melanoma was not thought to be linked to a genetic nerve sheath disorder, or at least it wasn't linked in our minds. If there was a link, there were no connecting the dots yet. There were some discussions of Pete's tumors being genetic, but not hereditary.

JOURNAL
DATE: April 4, 1992
DISTANCE: 2.2 miles
WEEK 26: Up 20 lbs.
NOTES: Ran to the end of Riverside Dive, walked back. Feels like the baby is bouncing from my chest to my pelvic bone!

Perhaps the introduction to this book could have read, "I should have been a doctor." Well, maybe not a doctor, but someone in the health field. It's crazy when you know more than your doctor. And I'm writing this looking back when there was no access to the internet. During my second pregnancy, I would visit with a different obstetrician in the practice at each checkup. Each time I would ask the attending doctor, "Are you sure there aren't two babies in there?" I got the same response every time: "No."

During my first visit, I had told the doctor that a history of twins ran in my family. After hearing only one heartbeat, he tried to assure me that there was only one baby inside. At the second visit, I told the doctor how nothing could satisfy my hunger, unlike my first pregnancy. This doctor's reply was that no two pregnancies are the same. At the next checkup, I said I felt movement on the top and bottom of my belly at the same time. I was sure the baby couldn't be that long at four months. This doctor told me it was gas. At my five-month checkup, I complained of the same symptoms my mother had when she carried twins. The doctor told me to wear tight panty hose to keep the varicose veins from looking like a sci-fi movie down below. (OK, that was Pete's description, not the doctor's, when I asked Pete if everything looked normal down there.) BUT the panty hose was the medical advice I was given by the doctor!

Then, FINALLY, at my six-month checkup, the sixth doctor said, after he noted my abnormal weight gain, "I'm going to order an ultrasound. Either we miscalculated your due date, or there are two babies in there." Three days later I had the ultrasound and was advised to take it easy because I was six centimeters dilated, and I was carrying twins! Three days later, on April 20th, I drove myself to the hospital again, but this time I knew I was in labor. And again, Pete missed witnessing the birth of his children, but through no fault of his own. The doctors didn't let him in the surgery room because they weren't sure if one or both babies would survive.

None of Pete's prior surgeries prepared me for what happened next. After my emergency horizontal and vertical C-section, the doctor on call asked if I wanted my tubes tied before he sewed me back up. I asked instead if my babies were going to make it. The doctor said he wasn't sure. I told him that having my tubes tied was something I'd have to discuss with my husband, especially since I only had heard one baby cry. I asked again why I didn't hear the second baby cry when they lifted her out of my abdomen. No one answered me, but one of the doctors briefly showed me my daughter and took her away with her brother.

That was the last I saw of her for a week. The birth of my twins was not the joyous occasion most parents get to experience.

I remember feeling sorry for my second twin, Dana—not for myself—when the neonatologist, Dr. Uma Sundarum, told me Dana would have either cerebral palsy or be mentally challenged. I knew other people felt sorry for me, but all I could think about was the life poor Dana would lead with physical or mental disabilities. I said to myself, "OK, I'm going to be the parent of a child with special needs," and that was the end of my self-pity.

While others turned to prayers, I turned to doctors. At the age of twenty-nine, I didn't know anyone who had gone through what I was faced with. Every time a doctor would ask me for consent to do another procedure on Dana's tiny body, I would ask Dr. Sundarum what she would do. As the mother of a son, Dr. Sundarum told me she had always wanted a daughter. She looked after Dana like she was her own. While I was recovering down the hall, Dr. Sundarum put a cot in the neonatal intensive care unit and slept next to Dana in her isolette incubator. Dana was wired to a jet ventilator that pumped air into both of her collapsed lungs to keep her alive. One night I was awakened from my morphine-induced sleep by the medical staff who wanted my consent to transport Dana to another hospital that was better equipped to save her life. Dr. Sundarum is the one who talked me through what was happening.

Was it prayer keeping Dana alive, or was it my superb insurance plan that enabled Dana to be transported to the NICU at Jersey Shore Medical Center? There she received nine spinal taps to relieve the hydrocephalus level 3 on her brain.

I felt disconnected from Dana while I recovered in a different hospital with her tiny twin brother, who was suffering from his own premature ailments. I shook my head in disbelief when the doctors told me that the black patches around my son's eyes could be permanent birthmarks from the traumatic birth he endured, which also could have caused possible hearing loss. I felt sorry for him. I could handle it, but I didn't want my son, Sam, to go through life that way. He had his whole cruel life ahead of him.

When I was finally released from the hospital, I went directly to see Dana. The nurses were happy to meet me after a week of tending to another motherless child at the NICU. They told me how pleased

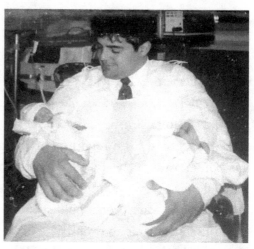

Pete in the neonatal intensive care unit holding the twins before Dana was taken to another hospital. Dana is on the left and Sam is on the right.

they were that someone from my family came to the hospital every day to hold and feed Dana. As I looked around, I thought to myself, *There can't be a God because prayers obviously are not working for all these "crack" babies with enlarged skulls.* I wondered what type of life these poor children were going to live once they were released from the hospital. They were already off to a bad start before entering the real world. Again, I did not feel sorry for myself for the life I was about to lead. I felt for these other babies who were not as fortunate as Dana, whose insurance was paying for the helicopter on the hospital roof, ready to transport her to New York University Hospital where the top surgeons in the world would put a permanent shunt in her head to stop the bleeding in her brain. Luckily Dana started to relieve the bleeding in her brain on her own and did not need the shunt. Miraculously, at the same time Sam's black eyes faded. I believe it was due to the telepathic way some twins can communicate.

Once I was released from the hospital, I had no choice but to fall into my new daily routine: drive to Point Pleasant, drop Paula off at my mother's house, and visit Sam at Point Pleasant Hospital. After spending time with my son, I would then drive to Jersey Shore Medical Center and visit Dana.

Pete would visit our twins after work, then spend what little time was left in the evening with Paula while I hooked myself up to an industrial breast pump and sat like a cow, pumping milk to bring to each hospital the following day. My routine changed up a month later when Sam was released from the hospital. We also had another addition to our house, a nurse. Insurance deemed Sam well enough to leave the hospital on a heart monitor, but not well enough to be left alone, or at least not in my care. Sam would spend four hours a day in the nurse's care. I used this time to drop Paula off at my mother's house and visit Dana. With what little free time I had, I used to play a game: matching medical bills with the explanation of benefits. Little did I know this was the beginning of a large compilation of medical files.

Several weeks later Dana was permitted to come home, also with a heart monitor, a nurse, and a list of directions. It was time for me to adjust my mental squares. I inadvertently redecorated my house in hospital décor. The kitchen held the medical supplies, along with charts and medical appointments for each baby and who was "working" what shift with what patient. The dining room was my administrative office. The dining room table housed organized piles of medical tests, results, bills, EOB's receipts, and more for both Sam and Dana. Dana's pile was a tad larger than Sam's. Upstairs were two nurseries: one room for Sam and Dana, and the other for Paula, who was only nineteen months old when she abruptly got a lot less attention.

The twins were closely monitored by different specialists for different developmental disabilities for the next two years. During this time, I told myself I would have to be the best parent possible. I distinctly remember Pete reading an article at that time about how divorce is higher in parents of children with disabilities. When he showed it to me, I said, "Oh, no. Not us. We're going to stick together and work through this." And that is what we did. I thanked everyone for their prayers during this time, but I thank Dr. Uma Sundarum for keeping my twins alive. Sam and Dana proved to be miracles, as they both overcame every disability they were born with.

TRAINING LOG
DATE: 5/10/96
WORKOUT: Pete and I did a half-mile warm-up, lifted 3 sets of 15 chest, back, bi's, and tri's, no rest. Six 20-yard sprints with 10 push-ups after each, and a half-mile cool down
NOTES: Good/tough; Upped weight on bi's to 30-lb dumbbell curls

To keep what little sanity I had left, I worked part-time, not so much for the money but to get out of the playroom in my house. I was lucky to get a part-time job in Lorstan Studio's high school sports department, which allowed me to mix my love for sports with my passion for photography This creative outlet led me to start my own business, Glory Days Sports Photography—but not for long. I was blindsided, and not by a linebacker.

Pete and I never saw the next hit coming. This one earned Pete his medical degree. OK, he didn't get his doctorate, but he knew more about what was happening on the inside of his body than the primary care doctor could see on the outside. He convinced his doctor to order more tests. Pete knew the bleeding he was experiencing was not due to hemorrhoids, and the surgeon confirmed that when he removed fifteen feet of Pete's small intestine due to an intra-abdominal tumor. The pathology report confirmed that Pete had a malignant sarcoma called a leiomyosarcoma, a rare cancer that grows around organs such as the stomach, bladder, and intestines.

Before Pete awoke from the first of his three surgeries, I was already on the phone trying to find a doctor that could reverse the colostomy bag. I tried my best to lessen the blow by telling him about the specialist I found in the Midwest. Fortunately, this doctor could reverse the bag, but as he told me, "His life won't be the same. He won't be able to digest food properly." Hearing this, all I could think was, *Well, Doc, life won't be the same with a bag either.*

27

The operation would have to wait, though. Pete needed another surgery, followed by a year of treatment to try to save his life. Dr. Jane Alavi and her assistant Jane Brashi at the University of Pennsylvania Hospital became Pete's saviors, just as Dr. Uma Sundarum was to Dana when she was fighting for her life. Because Pete was young and strong, the team at Penn Towers decided to bomb him with very strong chemotherapy and radiation for a year.

I fell back into my routine of driving to and from a hospital and deciphering medical bills. This time my mother came to my house to watch my children. When she couldn't be there, Pete's mother, Nonna, could. She even bought a house down the street, "just in case." We all knew what that "just in case" meant.

During the four-hour round trip to the hospital, I learned to appreciate each day and make the best of it. I enjoyed watching the leaves turn in the fall, stopping along the way at the Red Top Market for mums, and walking next door to the competition, Green Top Market, for apples. I looked forward to these small things. I was alone with my own thoughts. I dug deep to find the positive and stay that way. I told myself that I would expend the same amount of energy dwelling on the negative as I would on the positive. It was all the same amount of time in the car. Years later I read a quote by Art Buchwald that reminded me of my daily drive: "Whether it's the best of times or the worst of times, it's the only time we've got." Grit helped keep my family together during this time, just as it did when the twins were born.

Through all this I learned that you need more than great doctors and good insurance. You also need a sense of humor. Nothing about a serious illness is funny, but you can make fun of it. I wouldn't mock others, only myself. You must tread easy with your sense of humor when it comes to other people's feelings. I tried my best to never let Pete nor my children see me upset. Like an opponent, you should only show them your strengths and never your weakness. I never discussed the ticking time bomb.

You have to make the best of each situation or you won't get a chance to enjoy your life. You must remember that things will get better just as they got worse. Sometimes you can have a bad spell for a month, or for a year or two. During this time, do not dwell on the negativity. Face adversity, and be aware of it, but do not let things you can't control bring you down.

4

THE THREE MOST DREADED WORDS

TRAINING LOG
DATE: April 4, 2001
DISTANCE: 20 miles
TIME: 3 hr 2 min
NOTES: Last long run with Pam before marathon. Ran part of the course.
Windmill Hotdogs after!

I have learned to appreciate the good days. Most people just comment on having a bad day. Good days are not seen as joyous milestones. But every day you are alive and nothing out of the ordinary happens is a good day in my book, or maybe I should say, in this book. And at this time in my life, I was having good days. Other than the removal of his spleen due to another tumor, Pete was in very good health. (Remember, my definition of good health may differ from the average person's definition—just as my definition of a bad day may be different than the average person's.) My bad days seem to appear anywhere from one to five years. I never became too complacent because I knew the pattern.

While my children were in school, I worked part-time for the Borough of Pine Beach as their municipal alliance coordinator. It was a fantastic job, and I loved it! I planned and facilitated events for all ages through a grant from the Governor's Council on Drug and Alcohol

Awareness. Yes, I realize I'm contradicting what I previously wrote about partying, so let's just say now that I'm all grown up, I have a lot of experience in the field. Of the nine events I planned throughout the year, my favorite and most popular event was the Pine Beach 5K and One Mile Riverside Run. Pine Beach had never hosted a race until the Mayor asked me to direct a race to celebrate the town's 75th anniversary.

The race was to be part of the Diamond Jubilee festivities for 2000. However, I started planning the race in 1999 and decided to do a trial "run" that year. To everyone's surprise, over 440 participants showed up for the inaugural event. Mayor Corby and I decided we needed a separate committee to keep this event alive year after year. We solicited the help of friends and neighbors with specific talents that could enhance each aspect of the race. That committee was run like a Fortune 500 company, but with a lot of laughter at our monthly meetings. We all had great communications skills. We talked, we listened, and we understood; these are the fundamentals of any good relationship, be it business, friendship, or marriage. I wish every job could be run the way we ran the Pine Beach 5K. More people would enjoy their jobs, and in turn do well for themselves and their employers. I distinctly remember a conversation with a committee member as to how long I was going to keep doing this labor of love. My answer was, "Until it isn't fun anymore."

Everyone on the Pine Beach 5K race committee excelled at their job. My best friend, Pam, a former president of Ocean Running Club, was one of my two assistant race directors. The other assistant was my good friend, runner, and another past president of Ocean Running Club, Lee Pelton. Lee is a CPA, so he kept our books too. Runner and attorney Larry Perlberg not only gave us legal advice, he also oversaw the beautiful 3.1 mile course that ran along the Toms River and looped around the town on a bike path. Runner and IT expert Brian Downie took care of our website while assisting Larry. Pine Beach Borough Clerk

Charlene Carney and Pine Beach Councilman Chris Boyle took care of all town and county permits, paperwork, and anything else along those lines we would need. Runner and builder Rudy Rinderer secured our sponsors from his local business connections. Another former Ocean Running Club president, the late racewalker Al Hayden, was in charge of the One Mile Riverside Run and all racewalkers. Friend and neighbor Janet Addesso oversaw the volunteers, which eventually grew to over one hundred on race day.

If you're wondering why I am naming the entire race committee, it is because not only did they all work relentlessly for ten years on this race to help make it the largest and best 5K event in New Jersey, we all became good friends. They deserve the recognition. By its tenth anniversary, the race had over sixteen hundred participants from all over the world. It was designated a United States Track & Field NJ Masters Championship 5K Race, had a beginner's running program, donated all the proceeds to local charities, and started a scholarship program at Toms River High School South. It was a pleasure to hear how this race helped others, whether from a monetary standpoint or from the physical fitness aspect of training.

This part-time job allowed me to spend a lot of time with my family. It fit perfectly into one of the boxes in my life. Family was a large box. Dates with my husband consisted of stopping for something to eat after checkups for the removal of a neurofibroma on his head. A year later he had another nerve sheath tumor removed from his leg; these had the potential to turn malignant.

When Paula, Sam, and Dana came home from school, my box expanded to fit as much time as necessary helping my children with their homework and driving them to activities. The girls spent their youth collecting regional and national awards on the Toms River South Raiders Pop Warner Cheer Squad. I became so involved volunteering for the Pop Warner program that the Eastern Region Pop Warner Association gave me the Volunteer of the Year Award in 2004. I enjoyed spending this time with my entire family. I say "family" because Pete also volunteered by coaching Sam's Pop Warner football team. Toms River was known for many things, including a strong Pop Warner program, and Sam's team followed suit by winning a regional championship.

When Paula and Dana weren't cheering, they were taking tennis lessons. By the time they were in high school, they both traded their pompoms for tennis rackets and started to garner awards in that sport too.

Pete with Paula after winning her first of two high school tennis championships.

I'm proud to say, or maybe boast, that Sam was quite the athlete too. Besides football, Sam excelled in wrestling, but his favorite sport by far was lacrosse. He made the varsity squad his freshman year of high school, and he was the captain of the team his sophomore, junior, and senior years of high school. Sadly, his athletic career was sidelined by two knee surgeries. Fortunately, I was an expert in dealing with medical maladies, finding top-notch treatment, and navigating insurance documents with companies. I was hardly fazed when Sam was hit during football and it resulted in a torn right ACL.

During Sam's surgery, Pete became a caregiver for the second time in his life. The first was a few years earlier when his mother, Nonna, became ill. However, all the caregiving knowledge Pete and I had accumulated over the years could barely prevent his mother's quick demise.

Nonna, a quintessential Italian grandmother, loved cooking and spending time with her family, especially her grandchildren. We all loved her cooking and being around her bubbly personality. Nonna and I immediately connected the first time Pete brought me home to meet his parents. From the minute I dismounted Pete's motorcycle, she welcomed me like a daughter. I sat down to a dinner of delicious meatballs, which rivaled my own grandmother's.

The aroma and taste of Nonna's meatballs[1] brought back the only childhood memory I had of my dad's mother. My father and I would visit her after church on Sunday. I vaguely remember running through her small backyard in East Orange, New Jersey. She had rows of rosebushes. I would run up and down each row before going into the kitchen of the duplex home she shared with my Aunt Millie and cousins Len and Dianna. My grandmother would be at the stove cooking meatballs. I would eat them hot out of the pan before she added them to her gravy. Yes, gravy. Not sauce. If you add meat to a sauce, it is called GRAVY! That is a fact; end of discussion. My grandmother immigrated from Sicily, so it's true. Don't argue with me. I'm Sicilian.

There was another dish that Nonna cooked that brought back childhood memories, but not good ones. At least not good culinary memories: turkey dinner. I never knew what turkey was supposed to taste

[1]Note: this and other recipes can be found at the end of the book.

like until I had Nonna's moist turkey. Remember, my dad was a high school football coach. On Thanksgiving morning, my mom would put the turkey in the oven, and off we would go, bundled up in layers, to the Annual Thanksgiving Day game. The only thing worse than an un-basted turkey was a silent dinner. The outcome of the game set the tone for our holiday. If Bloomfield High School won, our house was filled with the laughter of assistant coaches celebrating their victory. If the team lost to their longtime rival, Montclair, we sat and ate dry turkey in silence.

This memory brings me to another turkey dinner I ate in silence: Christmas Day 2003. When Pete, the children, and I arrived at Nonna's house that holiday, we were shocked to find the dinner preparations had not yet begun. Nonna was just standing quietly at the sink. She didn't answer when we asked her what was wrong. Her unusual demeanor progressively got worse as we started to cook the turkey. The next morning Pete drove his mother to the local emergency room where an MRI showed a brain tumor. She didn't understand that she was going to need surgery. We had a hard time comprehending that she had a glioblastoma, a fast-growing, malignant form of cancer. The doctors said that with chemotherapy, she might survive four months in a semi-vegetative state. Without treatment, she might survive a month. Pete's father opted for the latter.

I spent that last month sitting by Nonna's bedside while my children were in school. When Nonna would get an occasional visitor, I'd relocate to the front porch of their riverside home and look out at the Toms River. The river was peaceful that winter month, slow and silent yet cold and lonely, and it reflected the steady decline of Nonna's health. It was there, on the front porch that I had one of my first precognitions of death. I was listening to the radio when a flock of seagulls flew over the water and gradually ascended into the gray sky at the same time Bob Dylan's "Knocking on Heaven's Door" came on. That night Pete and I decided we should bring our children over to see their grandmother for the first time since her surgery—and for the last time. The next morning, just five weeks after her diagnosis, she passed, we believe happily.

After Nonna's death we had many unanswered questions. Could her death be related to her sister's death? Aunt Connie, the mother of Pete's late cousin Gary, died in 1993, just fifteen months after her son's death. Did Aunt Connie pass from a broken heart or from cancer?

TRAINING LOG
DATE: September 9, 2008
DISTANCE: 3 miles
TIME: 25 minutes
NOTES: Ran in Winding River Park with Brian and the dogs. Fell again, twice.

Remember when I mentioned I didn't want to be doing the Pine Beach 5K when it wasn't fun anymore? Going into the tenth year, I knew it would be my last. I still enjoyed it, but not quite as much. Volunteers do not have a long shelf life, and I could tell my committee was ready to spend their free time elsewhere. I didn't blame them; I was ready too. I wanted to spend more time with Pete planning our new home on the sixteen acres of land we bought in Maurice River, New Jersey. I also wanted to spend more time planning my new venture: opening a running and tennis specialty store in downtown Toms River. Hit and Run Sports was a much-needed store in Ocean County, New Jersey.

There was something else that made the Pine Beach 5K a little less enjoyable: my health. I was constantly battling a cold. At first I thought it was allergies. I was always feeling run down and tired. Pete kept teasing me that my increasingly slow race times were due to my age. I didn't take that well. I wondered why I was slowing down at a quicker rate than my peers in the same age group. I was constantly injured, and worse, it took me longer than usual to recover. As a lifelong runner, I was very tuned into my body. I knew something was wrong, and so did my running partner Brian Downie.

Brian was a very fast runner. I would train with him on his long, slow days. He would run the several miles to and from my starting location. His slow pace was my fast pace. I would do a hard, short run on those days. One of our favorite places to train was at the then "Future Home of Jakes Branch Park" in Beachwood, New Jersey. It was over four hundred acres of undeveloped land where I could let Blue and Red, my two wild Australian Cattle Dogs, off leash while Brian and I would run trails cut by illegal ATVs. This was the first place I took a fall—not merely tripped and fell, but just fell straight down to the ground. I didn't know what happened. I think I blacked out for a moment and came to on the ground. Brian turned around and saw me laying there. He ran back to see if there was anything on the path that would have made me collapse. Nope. The second time this happened was in Winding River Park in Toms River, another place I would meet up with Brian to train. This time I fell twice, or maybe I should say, blacked out twice. Brian decided he was no longer going to run with me when it happened yet again, this time along the boardwalk in Pine Beach. This was the wakeup call in my head that I listened to. I knew it was time to tell my doctor, and not just because I sprained my ankle on the fall.

My primary care doctor did not diagnose anything out of the ordinary during a regular checkup. He was very concerned that I couldn't recall why I fell several times, though, so he referred to me to a neurologist. The specialist did not find anything either. I always find it humorous when a brain specialist says they don't see anything. Is that bad or good? The neurologist was also alarmed that I didn't remember how I fell, so she ordered more advanced CBC bloodwork.

My primary care doctor called to give me my results. The only thing I can remember from our conversation were the words *blood disorder, blood disease, hepatitis, AIDS,* and *blood cancer.* Not only did I need more tests, but I needed another set of ears to sit in the exam room with me and absorb the entire consultation. Pete was very upset and clearly not ready to be my caretaker. He said, "I'm the one who is supposed to get sick, not you." My sister Sue came along on my next doctor visit.

Overnight I transformed into a human pin cushion. A series of blood tests leaned toward a blood cancer, possibly multiple myeloma. Multiple what? Cancer of the plasma cells. I had never heard of it before. My doctor explained that plasma cells are an important part of the immune system. They produce and release antibodies, called immunoglobulins, to help fight infection. When you have abnormal or malignant plasma cells, you are susceptible to infections. These cells eventually take over the bone marrow, leading to soft spots in the bone called lytic lesions, where bone pain and fractures can occur. Another complication is kidney failure. However, I was very familiar with the next word I heard: *oncologist*. To be more specific, I was told to see a hematology oncologist.

To confirm I had multiple myeloma, I would need one of the most painful tests in the entire universe—and no, I'm not exaggerating. Ask anyone who has ever had the dis-pleasure of having a bone marrow biopsy, and they will agree with me 110 percent. I will try my best to describe the procedure, but I know I can't do the agony justice:

1. You lay sideways on a gurney.
2. The doctor numbs your hip so you do not feel the drill—yes, drill—break your skin.
3. As the doctor goes deeper you begin to feel pain, as the doctor only numbed your skin. As the drill keeps penetrating, the pain gets more intense. All this time you can't move, so you clutch the gurney rails.
4. When the doctor hits the bone, you hit the roof. The drill then does exactly what a drill is supposed to do: it drills a hole in your hip bone until it hits the center, the marrow.
5. The doctor then tells you to take a deep breath because the worst is about to happen. You're thinking, *How can this get worse?* But

it does: the drill extracts the marrow, not once, but twice. Wait, there's more: the drill somehow transforms into an excavator and takes a piece of your bone too!

6. Then the drill gets switched in reverse, and you feel the pain all over again as the medical grade Black & Decker tool makes its way back out.

I have had this procedure done twice. Both times I was never given an explanation as to why there is no anesthesia or pain medication administered. The second time they had me lie on my stomach. I think they did this so my scream was muffled into the pillow. However, my fingernails scratching the hospital wall made up for it.

The first time I had the procedure, the following week I reported to the doctor's office for the results. It's always bad news when you have to see the doctor in person. If everything is good, the doctor's office will just call you over the phone. Nothing prepares you for the three most dreaded words in the English language—and I don't mean "I love you."

It was very surreal to hear the oncologist say, "You have cancer." I went home, closed the box on Hit and Run Sports, and replaced it with a permanent box titled multiple myeloma. Since I never heard of this blood cancer before, I began researching everything I could on plasma cells. I looked up everything on white blood cells and how long multiple myeloma patients are expected to live. I also looked into treatment options, and which doctors were best. I wanted to talk to at least one, if not two, multiple myeloma specialists. I couldn't rely on the internet for everything.

Luckily, I live within hours to some of the best hospitals on the East Coast, one being Hackensack Hospital, where one of the top multiple myeloma doctors resided. Over the next several weeks, this doctor did more tests to see how far along the cancer was. His recommendation was to start chemotherapy right away since I was so young and "healthy." But if I was "healthy," why did I need to start chemo? Weren't there any other options? Not according to this doctor. Not only did I want another opinion; I *needed* another opinion.

I had to wait three months to see the top multiple myeloma specialist in the world. In December Pete accompanied me on my initial visit to Dr. Edward Stadtmauer (Dr. S) at the University of Pennsylvania Hospital, a place we were very familiar with. When we arrived, we had to wait three hours to see him. All I can say about the wait is that every second was worth it. He looked at my tests results, he looked at me, and he said, "Get out of here. I'm not treating you until you need it. Your blood is beautiful. Keep doing what you're doing, and I'll see you back here in three months." Of course, I had prepared a long list of questions including two of the utmost importance: Could I still run and was I allowed to drink wine? His response was yes to both. Bingo, this was the doctor for me!

Notice I didn't ask how long I had to live. I didn't have to. Dr. S explained to me that I was in the smoldering stage, the precursor to stage one. Some people can stay in this smoldering stage for more than thirty years; some are not so lucky. There was no way to know how long I had it, nor how long before it would progress. Dr. S said he would closely monitor me every three months. During this stage I would have a lower-than-normal immune system that had the potential to lead to other complications therefore I would have to take certain precautions. He told me about the different treatment options available—none of which included chemotherapy.

At some point every cancer patient wonders, *Why me?* and *How did I get this?* To this day I still question if it came from the high radon present in sections of Glen Ridge. Or did I use too much Round Up when I worked on our property in Franklinville? Was my well water in Franklinville contaminated by Pioneer Metal Finishing Inc., located 5.6 miles away? Did I run under the high-power lines too many times? Had I accidentally run through a superfund site all those days I ran in the backwoods of Bayville, New Jersey, with my dogs? It seemed ironic that Red Dog was diagnosed with a blood cancer, too, while Blue Dog got melanoma, as did his master, Pete. My hypothesis was and still is the Cherry Hill Inn. As I mentioned, for three years I worked in the basement of this grand old hotel. My office, as well as the back hallways, had exposed pipes on the ceiling that would often drop debris, especially when they were accidentally hit, which they often were when I transported the audio-visual equipment through the basement. Asbestos is also thought to cause multiple myeloma. A few co-workers have since died of various cancers, and who knows how many may still have or will get cancer.

Just like the three words *I love you* can change your life, so can the three words *you have cancer*. And those three words certainly did change my life, but not for the worse. If I wanted to beat cancer, I would have to make tactical changes in my life. Cancer is a war made up of a series of battles—some you win; some you lose. However, my goal was to win the war, and in order to win the war, I had to be strategic. I had to prepare on all fronts. I had to get in the best shape of my life, physically and mentally, just like I would for a race.

5

WARP SPEED

TRAINING LOG
DATE: February 2, 2009
DISTANCE: Approx 4 miles
TIME: n/a
NOTES: 2 loops around the resort

After my cancer diagnosis, I vowed I was going to live by Pete's motto: "Cancer may take years from my life, but I won't let it take the life from my years." And that is what we both did. That winter we took our children on our biennial trip to the Caribbean. This time something was very different, and not because of me.

Pete and I had a routine on our vacations. We would wake up before the children and work out. He would swim in the sea while I went for a run. We would plan to meet up at a certain time in a designated location, then wake the children for breakfast. However, I noticed Pete was finished swimming every day before I was done with my run. It was not that I was running slower and didn't make it to our rendezvous spot on time. He wasn't even waiting where the running path met the beach. Instead, every morning he would be asleep in a hammock that hung between two palm trees in the white sands of Jamaica. He swam, but not for as long as he planned. He told me he was simply too tired.

When we returned home, Pete confided in me about something he found in his groin area. He didn't want to worry me during our vacation about what he described as a lump no larger than the size of a small gold-foiled chocolate Easter egg. Given his history, we both knew he would need to see a doctor ASAP.

We were disappointed to find out his beloved oncologist, Dr. Jane Alavi, and her dedicated assistant, Jane Braschi, had both retired. Even the Penn Tower offices were gone. Pete was referred to a new oncologist at the all-new Abramson Cancer Center at UPenn. Yes, I'm so familiar with the University of Pennsylvania Hospital that I will now start referring to it like a local: UPenn. (The locals also refer to the hospital next to UPenn as CHOP: Children's Hospital of Pennsylvania, the saddest place on earth.)

Pete immediately had the mole next to the lump removed for a biopsy. The pathology results of this mole, that never once saw the sun in its entire forty-plus-year existence, was melanoma. We were baffled by these results, but we were more focused on what we had to do next. I say "we" because once again we would fight this battle together. I rearranged the boxes in my life. There was no time for me to be a patient. I now had to be a caregiver.

The doctors ordered an MRI of Pete's entire body before surgery to remove the lump. The image happened to be hanging on the end of his gurney along with his medical charts. We both were very well versed in reading test results, and this image showed yellow, orange, and red throughout Pete's entire body. He turned to me before being wheeled into surgery and said, "I'm screwed."

It turned out that this little mole had very long roots. These roots were long enough to reach the lymph nodes in the groin. Those lymph nodes, like all lymph nodes, had wires attached to them that go throughout the human body. They are there to carry good stuff around, but if cancer hits one of them, it carries the bad stuff too. In Pete's case, it carried the melanoma. Very bad stuff.

But why melanoma? How did Pete get skin cancer? His new oncologist, Dr. Fecher, explained to us he didn't get skin cancer. Melanoma is in the nerve sheath family. If someone is predisposed to a condition called dysplastic nevia with severe atypia, a benign mole can turn malignant. Dysplatic nevia moles are graded mild, moderate, and severe. Sometimes severe moles turn malignant. This one did.

After the surgery, the doctors were very optimistic. They explained that, with treatment, Pete could live ten to fifteen years. That seemed like a lifetime. We had no doubt that Pete would once again beat cancer. So, once again the chemotherapy treatment began, and we went on with life as we knew it.

That spring we continued with our plans to build a home in Maurice River. We attended Sam's lacrosse games, took the girls to tennis lessons, and boated on the weekends. Pete was healthy enough to drive himself to UPenn every day after work for treatment. Life was good.

At Pete's monthly checkup, we were informed that the cancer was spreading more quickly than anticipated. Although the news wasn't good, Pete was fine with it. The doctors cut his survival time to five to ten years. Pete always said he didn't think he'd live past forty-five, so he was very pleased that the doctors now predicted he could live well into his late fifties. That would give him enough time to see our children grow up and get married—and possibly play with his grandchildren by the pond on our property in Maurice River.

Those plans came to a quick halt the following month. We both had checkups with our oncologists on the same day at UPenn. Mine went well; Pete's did not. The doctor told us that melanoma is one of the most aggressive cancers in the world. They call it the great pretender because it has the potential to travel to other parts of the body and mimic other cancers. Often people are treated for the wrong cancer because the melanoma has disguised itself as different cancer. However, the doctors knew the cancer throughout his entire body, with the exception of the thyroid cancer they had also recently detected, was melanoma. The doctors were not concerned with the easily treated cancer of the thyroid gland. They were very concerned that the melanoma was not reacting to the chemotherapy. They told us Pete now had one to three years to live.

TRAINING LOG
DATE: August 12, 2009
WORKOUT: Ocean swim
DISTANCE: n/a
TIME: n/a
NOTES: Very bad. Felt weak.

Working out has always been a large box in my life. I believe you must take care of yourself, no matter what is happening in your life, and working out is one of the best things to do for your body and your mind. No matter what I am going through, I always make time to exercise. During the summer of 2009, I kept up with my triathlon training. Although swimming is my least favorite of the multisport endurance race, I knew I had to work harder at it because it was also my weakest. And when I say weakest, I mean I'm a very slow swimmer. There is no denying that I am one of the last participants to finish the swim. My only saving grace is that it is the first of the three sports, and I can make up a little ground on the bike, and a lot more on the run. I totally understand when people tell me they do not like running, because I can relate—I despise swimming. Regardless, like anything else I want to master, I had to work at swimming if I wanted to better myself in this sport. One hot August night I was trying to do that when I had my second forewarning of death—but not Pete's.

The Atlantic Ocean was not particularly rough that night, but the current was a little too strong for a weak swimmer. I was lagging far behind the others in the "group swim." Fellow Jersey Shore Running Club member and EMT Tina Duda noticed something was wrong; fortunately she never lets any swimmer out of her sight. I remember thinking that the seagulls looked so pretty as they flew low over the glistening ocean backlit by the setting sun. I felt very peaceful as I started to descend into the water. Tina quickly grabbed my arm and escorted me back to land.

I believe angels exist—but here on earth, as human beings. Tina was my angel that night, just as Dr. Sundaram was Dana's angel.

But where was Pete's angel? To look at him, you wouldn't think he needed one. You wouldn't think he was as sick as the doctors told us. After all, he was the only father that carried a mini fridge up six flights of stairs when the elevators broke during Paula's move-in day her freshman year at the University of Delaware. He hosted a clambake for his entire family after taking everyone boating on Labor Day weekend. He didn't act sick either, even though the doctors had just told us at his last checkup that he now had less than a year to live. After that checkup we stopped at Mikado, a Japanese steak house, to celebrate our twentieth wedding anniversary. Another typical date for us.

In September, the doctors coaxed Pete into having a genetic test performed, something he adamantly fought. Dr. Nathanson, the genetic specialist at UPenn, told us all the cancers he had during his lifetime were members of the nerve sheath family, and the doctors wanted to know if he had a heredity trait that is passed from generation to generation. I wanted to know that too. Pete did not. Given his family history, we knew what the results would be, but the doctors needed to confirm it. Pete and I made a deal. He agreed to have the test done if I promised I would never have our children tested.

It was no surprise to us that the test results showed that Pete lacked the gene, known as CDKN2A, to fight these malignant nerve sheath tumors. However, we were very shocked to hear that the doctors now said that they "hoped Pete would make it to Christmas."

With this horrific news, we both went on autopilot. He applied for disability, and I applied for a job, or maybe I should say, I was appointed a new job—a full-time job with much needed benefits. With a strong political connection, I immediately started to work for the

Ocean County Board of Elections, located just two-and-a-half miles from our house. My political connection was now my boss: George Gilmore, a powerful man who had a lot of compassion for those in need.

Working close to home fit perfectly into another box as it allowed me the time needed to take Pete to his daily radiation treatments at a nearby hospital. This treatment was not to eliminate the cancer; it was designed to relieve the pain from the pressure of an ever-growing tumor on his brain. The cancer not only had spread to this major organ, but to his lung as well. Pete dug deep to spend as much quality time with his children as possible. He attended all of Dana's tennis matches and even her end-of-the-season banquet. He accompanied me to visit Paula on parent's weekend at the University of Delaware, and he watched all but one of Sam's football games.

That October Pete was admitted into the hospital at UPenn. Our children, like everyone else, were bewildered. Pete still looked strong. One night after dinner with the twins, Dana asked me when her father was going to come home. As she put it, "He always beats cancer. What is taking so long this time?" That's when I did the hardest thing I've ever done in my life. I told my children that he wasn't going to get better this time. Dana collapsed on the floor, and Sam left the house. I called Paula. How I wished I could have been there in person to tell her about her father.

A few days later Pete was discharged from the hospital. The oncologist wanted to see Pete the following week. At that visit, Dr. Fecher informed us that we no longer needed to come back. With that, the doctor said, "We hope he can make it to Thanksgiving." Dr. Fecher told me privately that she wished the new proton therapy machine was ready; it was a new type of radiation treatment that could pinpoint cancer cells using high-energy beams. Perhaps that could have saved Pete's life. Instead I was given instructions to contact hospice.

When we returned home that afternoon, Pete gave me instructions too—instructions on how to do some things around the house that I never knew were needed. I took notes on chores I never paid much attention to. He laughed and told me I was "so screwed." We also went through important paperwork. I drove Pete to Maurice River, and we discussed his final wishes during his last visit to our property. I asked if he would like his remains spread in our pond. He joked and said, "No, because you will end up selling the property." He still had his sense of humor. He wanted his ashes to be placed next to our beloved dog Buggs' ashes on the bottom shelf of our curio cabinet.

Pete had another request. He wanted his hospice nurse to be a male. Holy Redeemer Home Care and Hospice assigned David Kohut to Pete's case. When David arrived that first week in November, I had to convince him how sick Pete really was. I explained to him that Pete was declining in rapid time. I also contacted family and close friends to tell them the same. Everyone wanted to see Pete. It made me wonder if some of those people were visiting Pete for their own sake or for his. So many people wanted to see him that David suggested scheduling visits with only those closest to Pete, as he should spend as much time with loved ones as possible. I agreed.

With a week to go before Thanksgiving, Pete could no longer walk. When David wasn't there to assist Pete, my son was. I would wake Sam in the middle of the night to help me carry his father to the bathroom. This is not something a teenage boy should ever have to do. Pete didn't want this either. One night his stubbornness got the best of him when he tried to make it to the bathroom alone and fell, splitting open his nose. I tried my best to use butterfly bandages where the stitches should have been.

Pete's stubbornness was also a blessing as he willed himself to keep going through Thanksgiving week. He waited for Paula to come home from college that Tuesday night. He waited for Sam to play in the Thanksgiving Day football game, the only game Pete missed that season. This stubbornness also kept Pete from sleeping in the hospital bed we had set up in the bedroom. He referred to it as his "death bed." He insisted on sleeping in a recliner in the corner of our bedroom instead.

I tried to keep Thanksgiving as normal as possible for our children. Although the ritual of Pete and I making our sweet potato soup was not going to happen, Toms River High School South made sure we still had a turkey dinner. Students dropped off a prepared meal. I took the food up to my bedroom, set a table, and we ate dinner together as a family. Pete's favorite football team, the Giants, were even playing on TV. Unfortunately, they lost to the Cowboys.

After dinner Pete asked me to help him get into the hospital bed. I knew what this meant. As his limbs got cooler, the children got more upset. They pleaded with me to get more blankets. I knew it wouldn't help, but I did it anyway. At midnight I told Paula, Sam, and Dana to say good night and goodbye to their father. I got into our bed, which was up against his death bed, and held his hand.

I awoke an hour before my 3:00 a.m. alarm, the next scheduled time I was to administer Pete's morphine. The room was quiet and still. I turned my head toward Pete until my eyes could adjust to the darkness. I did not see his chest rise and fall. There were no sounds of struggling breaths, there were no deep chest movements gasping for air. I laid my head on his motionless body and cried for three hours. At 5:00 a.m. I woke up my children and then called hospice. The nurse on call arrived at my house at 5:26 a.m. and pronounced Pete dead on Friday, November 27, 2009, just eight months after his diagnosis.

The funeral director at Carmona Bolen in Toms River gave me invaluable advice, as we planned Pete's service to best fit Pete's wishes and my family's best interest, not those, who as he put it, I "will not hear from again." He was correct. He was also right when he told me to accept everyone's help because if I didn't, they would stop offering. He went on to tell me that in time, not only would I not get help, but I would not hear from these people either. He was right again. However, there was one person who I would hear from—and still do. Pete's best friend, Rich Rifkin, promised Pete he would look after the kids and me. He has kept his word.

Rich summed up Pete's life perfectly in the eulogy he prepared. After hearing this well-written memorial, many people were only half-joking when they asked Rich to write a eulogy for them. He was that good. I told Rich he was too good, as he made Pete sound like a saint, and I knew better. In fact, Pete's legendary college football coach, the late Dick Wacker (yes, that was his real name), used to call me the saint. He referred to me as "Saint Sally" for putting up with Pete. Nevertheless, Rich captured Pete's spirit at the service when he spoke the following words:

Sally, Paula, Sam, Dana, Mr. Kalksma, Donna and Bob, Paul and Dorothy, friends, and fellow Pete Kalksma fans, when people think of Pete Kalksma, several traits come to mind:

Athleticism and toughness – Everyone who ever competed with or against Pete on an athletic field knows that they never saw anyone tougher. He was seemingly impervious to pain and had a dogged determination that became his philosophy in life. It was rare in his adult life to see the intensity and aggression that he brought to his athletic arenas, but when you saw it, it was a look that could melt ice, and God help the person who was on the receiving end of it. On the football field, *nobody* hit harder than Pete. (He *loved* to hit. As an adult, he lamented how much he missed "hitting people.") Pete was a tremendous natural athlete. Blessed with fantastic instincts and a tenacity that would be his trademark throughout his life, Pete found great success early on. He played linebacker and fullback in high school at Paramus High and then linebacker at Glassboro. He excelled in wrestling in high school, as a member of a legendary, undefeated PHS teams of the late '70s. After college, he came to love rugby. He achieved great notoriety in his athletic pursuits, gaining all-league honors and many accolades and recognition. Had Pete

51

been a step faster in the forty-yard dash, it wouldn't be far-fetched to envision a stint in the NFL as part of his resume. He was *that* good. He had a presence about him that made others want to be in his orbit. That is why it was an obvious choice for the coaches of those teams to name Pete team captain. And he took that title seriously. I can remember him calling out some teammates who weren't taking their responsibilities as seriously as he thought they should. He let them know it, in no uncertain terms. That is not an easy thing to do with your peers as a teenager. He was simply the toughest guy I ever knew. I never saw him really hurt. When there'd be scraps in high school, Pete was always the last one standing.

Work ethic – Pete felt there were no shortcuts in life. The quote he chose for our high school yearbook was so simple and so perfectly captured who he was. It said: "If you're going to do something, do it right, or don't do it at all." That was the way he lived every day of his life. Later, by the way, in our yearbook, in reference to an incident in which we got arrested for sleeping on the beach down the shore, he wrote the following inscription to me: "Don't let me sleep on the beach, or I'll let Mele breathe on you." Ah, that razor sharp wit we all loved.

Old school values – Pete saw things in black and white. There was very little gray in his world. I always joked with him that he was born forty years too late. His was a world in which you didn't buy things on credit, your word was your bond, and when you did a job, you worked as hard on it as you could, regardless of if you were feeling lousy or tired or unmotivated. He would be back at the office and working out in the garage the day after chemo.

That smile and that laugh – When I think of Pete, he has that easy smile on his face, and I hear that chuckle that was his trademark. It is what many people have mentioned to me as the enduring image of him even though they hadn't seen him in decades. That chuckle, by the way, was often used as a defense mechanism. If we were out somewhere and I saw Pete laughing in response to something that was said, I'd ask him later what was so funny. Most of the time, he'd say, "I have no idea, they were talking into my bad ear."

Humility – Despite having plenty of reasons to be full of himself, Pete was never vain. Blessed with good looks and a rock-solid body, he never strutted or preened. We were friends for nearly forty years, and I *never* heard him brag about himself. And when others would sing his praises, either to him or about him, he would just chuckle and shrug, and try to change the subject.

Fearlessness – Pete struggled with serious physical ailments his entire adult life. And yet I never heard him utter the "woe is me" mantra. He believed that you played the cards you were dealt, and you did the best you could. I never once saw fear in his eyes.

My name is Rich Rifkin, and Pete and I were best friends. Growing up, Pete's house was the center of our universe, in that it was the meeting place for all of us before we would head out for the evening. Partly this was due to the central location of the Kalksma's house on Dover Street in Paramus. But it was also because Pete's parents created such a warm and welcoming place for us. We'd all agree after school to "meet at Kalksma's at 7:00." Me, Vinny, Dennis, Brian, Schmelz, Maio, Kocses, Hennessy, Turk, Muni—we'd all arrive on time, and where would we find Pete? Asleep in his room. He always had to take his "nap," and we'd sit around waiting for him to shower, eat, get ready, and *then* we'd finally be able to go. He picked up one of his nicknames, "Speed," in those days because we *always* were waiting on Pete.

Pete's sister, Donna, two grades older than us, let us tag along to our first rock concert to see David Bowie at Madison Square Garden. And Pete's younger brother, Paul, made him laugh like no one else. They were each other's best audience. We'd kid Pete that Paul was a younger, better-looking, funnier, wittier version of him, and perhaps we should just hang out with him instead of Pete. He'd just beam with the pride of a big brother at that notion.

We had a magical time growing up. We did lots of things I wouldn't say we are proud of, but were for the most part harmless, and our days and nights were filled with great times. Our spouses and our kids have heard many of the stories ad nauseum, and they never get old. Those were good times, with lifetime friendships forming, the bond of our crew becoming as strong as a "band of brothers." We loved music, we loved cruising around town on our bikes, then later in our cars, and we loved just hanging out together. There is a very tight-knit group of us from those days that I'm proud to say is as close today as we were more than thirty years ago, and Pete was without a doubt, our leader, our heart, and our soul. He was the alpha dog. He was the kind of guy that the girls wanted to date and guys wanted to be around.

Pete loved Bugs Bunny growing up. So much in fact, that he later named his dog after the Rascally Rabbit. Pete's signature cheer of approval at sporting events became "That's the old pepper." Not everyone knows that he got that from one of his favorite episodes, "Baseball Bugs." In high school, Pete cruised through on his natural charm. One young female teacher took quite an interest in Pete's, ahem, schoolwork. He thought it was hilarious. After high school, Pete moved on to Glassboro State (now Rowan College) where in addition to his success on the football field, Pete earned his degree in Geography, but the most significant thing he found at Glassboro was the love of his life, Sally Cavallaro. As I've mentioned, Pete had never been one who had much difficulty with the ladies. And he was dating a few at Glassboro. But after he met Sally, that was the end of his "playing" days. They married in 1989, a few years after graduation, and remained devoted partners ever since.

Along the way, after graduation and trying to figure out what he wanted to be when he grew up, Pete made a living as a commercial diver, turning a hobby he and Vinny Feorenzo learned in high school into a vocation. *This* is a profession not for the faint of heart. Pete would don a leaky wet suit and dive into nasty, brackish, freezing water and repair whatever they were being paid to repair—bridges, barges, whatever. He did this for a few years, and it was during these years that Pete did some traveling, seeing parts of the world that he'd never been to: California, Europe, Central America. It proved to him something that he already knew about himself . . . he was a Jersey guy, a homebody, and Jersey was good enough for him. Seeing those places was interesting, but home was what was most important to Pete. He then settled into a very successful career that was easier on him physically and allowed him to utilize his natural gifts—a sales executive in the hot mix asphalt and paving industry.

Over the years we'd talk about once a week. You know you've been friends with someone forever when you greet a forty-eight-year-old man on the phone with "What's up, loser?" We'd talk about our lives, our families, our careers, and just shoot the bull. We'd find reasons to get together. Pete would come to my house to help me out with a variety of do-it-yourself projects. We played a lot of tennis and golf. It always drove Pete crazy that I was better than him at these "finesse" sports. I explained to him that you can't play football and wrestle at corporate events, so his days at the top of the athletic food chain were over. At that point, he'd punch me so hard in the arm that I could feel it two days later. He played tennis with Paula and Dana and was so proud when he couldn't beat them anymore. He'd lift weights in the garage with Sam and loved to brag about Sam's "guns" during football games.

As Pete's prognosis grew grim, I asked him if there were any "bucket list" items he wanted to check off, knowing full well what the answer was going to be. "All I wanna do is hang out and catch as many of the kids' games and events as I can." And that's what he did, enduring many long drives to catch Paula and Dana's matches and Sam's football games. He loved watching them play lacrosse, too, wishing we had that sport when we were in high school. All three of

Pete's kids are high achievers, being named captains of their teams and serving as leaders in their communities. The apple, obviously, has not fallen far from the tree. (I guess we'll give Sally a little credit for their success too.)

No one can really relate to the physical duress and challenges Pete endured for the last fifteen years. Yet he never complained, and he never let them define who he was. Because he never brought it up, it was easy to forget how physically uncomfortable he often was. But I know very few people who could have survived what he did. It was simply his indomitable spirit that refused to acknowledge or give in to his condition. His mindset was "If you ignore it, it can't win."

We could tell "Kalksma" stories all day here. There are that many. Legendary stuff. But he wouldn't be comfortable with that. He never liked being the center of attention. In fact, he is surely thinking right now, "All right, Rifkin, enough, wrap it up." So, I will.

Pete's life was a testimony to simple values: work hard, play hard, respect other people, keep your ego in check, actions count more than words, don't spend what you don't have, and most of all, love and cherish your family. He lived a wonderful life, and he leaves a great void. But his smile, his laughter, his love endures—and will for generations to come. He was a special man. A great husband, father, son, brother, and friend. The ancient Roman philosopher Cicero said: "The life given to us by nature is short, but the memory of a life well spent is eternal." I will miss him and think of him every day of my life.

6

THE BOP BAG

TRAINING LOG
DATE: December 7, 2009
WORKOUT: 5:00 a.m. - took each dog 2 miles
TIME: Slow!
NOTES: First thought when I woke up: Today is the first day of the rest of my life.

After taking the allotted three-day bereavement time off from work, I resumed my job at the Ocean County Board of Elections. Overwhelmed by the rapid changes in my life, I never had time to grieve. I was miserable, but missing my old life was not an option. It was not going to make my life better now. I knew if I kept thinking of the past, I would get depressed. I couldn't let all the "what ifs" consume me. Looking at the future would upset me too. This stress started to cause sleepless nights. I had to make my life better by concentrating on the moment, on the day, on the task I was doing. I didn't forget my past. I didn't stop planning for the future. I just didn't beat myself up with past regrets, and I didn't worry about what might happen. The ancient Chinese philosopher Lao Tzu summarized it best when he said, "If you are depressed, you are living in the past. If you are anxious, you are living in the future. If you are at peace, you are living in the present." Pretty good quote, huh? No wonder he's a famous philosopher.

The stairwell brought me peace. Yes, stairs are one of the two things that rescued me. You see, I felt like a caged animal working in the basement of an old government building. I was not used to sitting at a desk for eight hours a day. I remembered Pete telling me he felt the same way years earlier when he had a short-lived office job in Manhattan. He would run up the stairs during his break. I decided I would give it a try. I loved it. Soon I was using my thirty-minute lunch break every day to run up the stairs as many times as I could to relieve the stress and clear my mind

of bad thoughts. I swapped my desk chair for a stability ball and added "under the desk" bike pedals to my daily repertoire.

Stair workouts started to replace my running. I didn't have to get up for work an hour earlier to run, and I didn't have to try to squeeze in a few miles later in the evening. This new workout was enough to keep me in decent shape, even transform my body (especially my

Sitting on my stability ball at work; you can see my "under the desk pedals" to the right.

butt) by using a different set of muscles. The cardio was off-the-charts intense.

TRAINING LOG
DATE: March 30, 2010
WORKOUT: Stairs – did 5 floors 10 times at lunch
TIME: 28 – 31 seconds each
NOTES: Felt good

Sometimes life just throws you a lot of crap at one time—a lot of crap that you must pick up and dispose of. When you are hit with bad news over and over again, be it in one week, one month, or one year, I can honestly tell you it won't last. It may seem like it's never-ending because you can't see the end, but it will stop eventually. Hang in there. It may not turn out the way you plan, but you can make the best of the finish. You can even make the best of what you are going through. That's what I did when my family was bombarded with more illness and more deaths the year after Pete passed.

Inheriting my mother's lack of empathy when it comes to minor ailments could be a blessing. As a child, I was often left to fend for myself if I wasn't profusely bleeding to death. It puts a lot of things in perspective, like not raising wimps. However, I knew Sam was seriously hurt when he went down in a lacrosse game that spring after his father's death. It was just parental instinct. For the second time in two years, he needed surgery. This time it was his left knee with a torn ACL, MCL, and meniscus. It was the end of his athletic career, but not the end of the world.

That was a light hit compared to the next series of events. In September, Pete's father passed away, and my mother was diagnosed with esophageal cancer. I felt like an inflatable Bozo the Clown Pop Bag. Remember the life-size punching bag filled with sand on the bottom so it never went down? It only tipped. Every time that clown was punched, it would just wobble, then stand straight back up with a smile on its face. Yup, that was me. I was going to make the best of this crazy amusement park with roller coasters and clowns. I dared life to show me what was in store for tomorrow. I would take it. I would coach my children, no matter how old they were, that they must never give up. They must try their best to dodge each blow. When they couldn't, they must not fall. They must keep standing and fight back. They couldn't give in.

Here is something else I taught my children: It is wrong to talk bad about other people, and it is unethical to talk about other people's private business, including medical problems. Therefore, I am going to change some names in this book to tell you something important: I broke my promise to Pete and had my children tested for CDKN2A. Although I didn't need a genetic test to tell me which of my children inherited the same genetic disorder as their father, the doctors did. My three children knew they didn't need a lab in Gaithersburg, Maryland, to tell them if they lacked the gene to fight nerve sheath tumors. It would have been just as well since they didn't need that burden of knowing a definitive answer. All I had to do was look at my children to know who was positive and who was negative. I could see by their outer beauty and inner strength who would carry CDKN2A. Not having it was a curse too. For a little bit of their privacy in this book I will rename them Z, Q, and X.

Child X was me. As much as that child wants to deny it, that child also jokes about it to accept it, just as I would. Everything about X is me, but thankfully the good is 100x magnified on X. This child is a virtuous, caring person whose beauty is only outdone by the class and grace they possess. Child X is so driven, so smart, that sometimes it gets in the way.

Child Z looks like Pete and has since birth. You could interchange any school picture from grade school through high school and you would think you were looking at the same person, especially given Z's abundant presence of dysplastic moles. However, like X, Z was a better version of Pete. Z is smarter, kinder, and much more sensitive.

Child Q is Pete reincarnated. Q's personality, sharp cutting sense of humor, love of animals, boating, water, diving, and even the daily naps are exactly like Pete. When Q was younger, Pete would say, "Watch Q walk. Q walks like a linebacker. Q is a stud." That is and was Pete.

But a definitive answer was still needed so the doctors could follow all three children closely for the early detection of tumors. And the answer was exactly the results I predicted. Two of my three children tested positive for the same genetic trait as their father. I lied to Pete for the well-being of our children, something I don't regret. They were now *my* children.

And so, two of my children began their journey of ongoing tests at UPenn. When someone has a serious medical condition, I don't think they ever get off the roller coaster of ups and downs. This ride can be very scary at times, but my children learned to enjoy the ride. At one visit, my children amused themselves during a long wait for a full-body MRI by pretending to film horror movies in their hospital gowns. In the summer, some families would take their children on a day trip to Six Flags Great Adventure in nearby Jackson, New Jersey. We would go to UPenn. We would explore the area and find pretty gardens, beautiful sculptures, and good places to eat.

TRAINING LOG
DATE: January 14, 2012
WORKOUT: Stairs in NYC
TIME: 60 floors 3 times (11:26, 11:45, 11:21)
NOTES: Linda's friend's apartment building on 60th. Good, steep.

I learned to appreciate single parents more, and I mean real single parents, not divorced single parents. I mean the widows and widowers who have had to become both the mother and father to their children. This is extremely stressful. For instance, driving Sam and Dana 725 miles to college—dropping Sam off at Coastal Carolina and Dana off at the College of Charleston—was not as stressful as it was making the return trip solo. I used this time alone in the car to think about how I would now rearrange the boxes in my life.

During times of stress, I never turned to alcohol or drugs. Drugs only compound a problem, and I wanted to save the alcohol for some good times. Working full-time as a single mother did not afford me the time I needed to unleash all my pent-up anger. When I rearranged the boxes in my life to be a father, it left little time for me to work out. My solution was to just work out harder. Whatever spare time I found, whether it was thirty minutes or three hours, I devoted it to *me* and my well-being. I continued to use my thirty-minute lunch break to do a quick stair workout five days a week. Sometimes I would treat myself to a day in New York City with my best friend, Linda, who lived in Manhattan, for a more intense stair workout. She would sneak me into various buildings in the city to train in the stairwell. She would hold my warmups and be on the lookout for security, since most building superintendents do not allow strange middle-aged women to enter and run up the stairs as hard as they can. Just like our college days, I coaxed her into joining me in this mischievous act, only this time it was for a workout.

Stairs saved my life. Some people join self-help groups. Not me—I ran up the stairs, and in turn I found a great group that helped me. Or maybe I should say, they found me, and I helped them too. The Multiple Myeloma Research Foundation (MMRF) heard about my stair climbing and invited me to participate in the prestigious invite-only Empire State Building Run-Up (ESBRU). The MMRF is a nonprofit organization founded by a patient with a whole lot of grit, Kathy Giusti. When Kathy was diagnosed in 1998, the survival rate for multiple myeloma was only three to five years because there were not enough drugs on the market for this type of blood cancer. Kathy, a Harvard business grad (aka smart woman), did not like her diagnosis and decided to change it. She started the MMRF, which has now become one of the top cancer research nonprofit organizations in the world. Since its inception they have helped bring over twelve drugs through FDA approval, increasing the survival rates for many patients. If I sound like a spokesperson, that's because I am. I became one of the MMRF's strongest advocates, using my stair climbing to raise awareness and much-needed money to fund the research.

The MMRF was granted entry bibs to the ESBRU as their charity organization. Forget what I wrote earlier when I said ESBRU stands for the Empire State Building Run-Up. ESBRU really means Extremely Sadistic Body Racing Unnaturally. After I finished my first race of running up the stairs of the Empire State Building, I told the MMRF I wouldn't do it again—it was the hardest thing I ever put my body through. Defying gravity and running as fast as you can up eighty-six floors of steep steps in a dimly lit, dusty gray stairwell with no air, just jostling elbows away from other participants, was unfamiliar territory. When you exit the stairwell onto the observation deck, the gust of cold February night air restricts your lungs. Trying so hard to catch your breath as you see the finish line is very daunting. All of my prior training did not prepare me for the excelled heart rate by the twentieth floor, the pain that ran through my thighs by the time I hit the fortieth floor, and my trembling biceps from floor sixty on. Then there was the climber's cough that lasts for days, reminding you of every excruciating step to the top. Of all the races I have ever done in my life, this was by far the most difficult. The following year the MMRF asked me to participate in the ESBRU again. I said yes. I wanted to see if I could best my time from 2012 when I raced up the stairs in 19:35 minutes and placed third in my age group. Not bad for a rookie, if I must say so myself.

Like most everything I do, I did as much research as I could to perfect my form and increase my speed. I read up on stair climbing, also called tower running, and found more races I could enter. I was hooked.

I trained even harder for my second ESBRU for two reasons. I knew what I had to do to conquer that beast of a building, and I was hit with the hardest blow of my life. I wasn't prepared for what was to happen next . . .

When I picked the fax up off the machine at work and turned to walk back to my desk, my eyes went directly to my assaulter. I wasn't expecting such a horrible attack. I knew something bad was about to happen, but I didn't think it would be that brutal. There was a cold sharp pain in my chest as the knife entered and I read the word *neurofibroma*. My inner voice begged, "No, don't do this. Please stop." I couldn't get away. I saw the cold knife coming back again, and this time it hurt more: *schwannoma*. "No, if there is a God, then please make it stop." I continued pleading as I saw the knife coming faster and harder, straight for my heart: *sarcoma*. "Don't drop, Sally; stay strong and keep moving. Keep your eyes focused. Don't look at anyone." I picked up the pace without making a scene. I thought I was being nonchalant, but I felt my coordinator's eyes on me. I heard her call out my name as I swiftly left the office. I told myself to head for the stairs, just run. I knew no one could catch me once I hit the stairs. Again I heard my coordinator call my name when she entered the stairwell. I took the stairs two at a time just as I did in the ESBRU, past the exit for the first floor where anyone surely would have thought I exited to get fresh air. My mind was too numb to feel any pain from sprinting up past the second-floor exit for the cafeteria, then past the door for the third floor. I picked up the pace and passed engineering on the fourth floor. I knew I had one more floor until I could collapse on the roof. When I reached the top, I kept rereading Q's MRI results, sobbing. "No, Pete, you are not taking Q. You can't have Q. Q is mine now," I said over and over again.

You know what really sucks? When there is a detour to UPenn and you can navigate your way there through the back streets without turning on the GPS. That's not a bad thing; it just sucks that I've been to UPenn that many times. It's not like I graduated from this school, but I might as well have since I probably spent more time there than some of the residents, and I knew more than some of doctors back in

Jersey. In fact, if the local pediatrician listened to me seven months ago, I wouldn't have been driving Q back to the hospital for a follow-up instead of a consultation! You see, Q had a pain down the left thigh, a classic sciatic nerve symptom. The pediatrician, who preferred to boast about his latest swim than discuss Q's ailments, suggested that Q stop running. I asked for an MRI. He gave Q a script for an X-ray. I argued with him that the X-ray was not going to show us the problem. When I proved him wrong, he gave Q a month's supply of anti-inflammatories. It didn't help, so he gave Q a script for painkillers to take back to college. Not the smartest thing to do. I was furious that the pediatrician did not take into consideration that this child was predisposed to nerve sheath tumors. After six months of pain, Q finally got an MRI. Q was back at college and had to find an imaging center far from home. Q walked a mile one night, in pain, for the MRI, only to be turned down because Blue Cross/Blue Shield had given the wrong authorization code for an out-of-state procedure. Q returned the following week and had the MRI. That fax I received at work confirmed that I was right. Something was pressing on the sciatic nerve. Something bad. After I digested the news, I made Q an appointment at UPenn. And there we were, driving back to the Abramson Cancer Center when we hit a detour. Just like life.

The first office visit was a twisted reunion. It looked all too familiar when we got off the elevator. We were on the same floor as Pete's last oncologist. When we entered the waiting room, I said to myself, "Oh God, it's the same round-faced, orange-cornrowed receptionist with no personality." What was worse, everyone remembered me. When they looked at Q, their faces couldn't hide that the nightmare was real.

Q had surgery to remove two tumors, one of which was located on the base of the spine. The surgeon informed us that the tumor was in a tricky spot. It was growing on the part of the spine that controls the mobility in the lower half of the body. A nerve specialist would be assisting in the surgery to test Q's nerves as the tumor would slowly be removed. The entire tumor could not be removed without permanent loss of mobility on both legs. A compromise was struck during the surgery. The surgeon, Dr. Zagar, deemed that enough of the tumor was excised, leaving only nerve damage to the foot, just as Q's father had experienced years earlier.

During Q's recovery, I sat by Q's bedside every day and slept in that same chair at night. The view from room 936B overlooked Franklin Field. The window faced the open end of the massive concrete horseshoe-shaped stadium. I could see the last three red letters outlined in white against a blue turf: ENN. I had an uninterrupted view of the bleachers, where I remembered Pete and I sitting in 2007 when we watched Paula round the last turn to clock her fastest 400 to date. How can one place have a memory at each end of the spectrum? One of the proudest moments of a parent's life, especially if one parent happens to be a runner. A place where young top athletes from all over the country pursue their dreams to be the fastest, the strongest, the best. A stadium filled with pride encompassed by a track filled with hope.

I remember so clearly it was late April. It was the Penn Relays, and Paula was just a freshman when she made the 4 x 400 team for Toms River High School South. It was a continuation from her successful fall debut on the varsity tennis team, and just the beginning of her dreams. Life was good back then. Pete was healthy, and the kids were happy. That school year the twins reached the pinnacle of their Pop Warner career as Dana's cheer squad won the national title, and Sam's football team won the conference. Our children were getting good grades, and Pete made the right move by switching careers. He was on the board of directors for National Paving.

Did I appreciate it? Yes. Did I take it for granted? At times. Did I want my old life back? No. I couldn't let the past try to consume me. Those fond memories dropped like the thermometer outside on that damp March 12th evening while I sat next to Q. It was the thirty-second anniversary of my first date with Pete. Happy f*&%ing

anniversary. That date no longer meant the promise of a relationship. Instead, like Franklin Field, it held hope for the future. We will recover. We will heal. And we must persevere!

When I thought of the past, it was not with sadness but anger. I tried to put more pieces of the puzzle together. Did Q's prior diagnosis with vitiligo have anything to do with CDKN2A? Was Q's autoimmune deficiency the result of this genetic disorder? There was one piece that fit perfectly: Years earlier Z had a small lump removed from behind the ear, causing temporary loss of the vocal chords and permanent nerve damage, just like Pete.

Q recovered and returned to college. And just like Pete, another tumor appeared, but this time on Z. The tumor was on the leg, again, just like the one Pete had at that age. And so, history repeated itself, and we began the process all over again. Only now Q's medical box got smaller, while Z's got larger.

The courage and strength my children exhibited was admirable. They never complained. In fact, they, too, made the best of the situation by agreeing to be part of a study on CDKN2A. It was conducted by their genetic specialist, Dr. Nathanson, and Dr. Merill, from the Division of Translational Medicine and Human Genetics at UPenn, along with their dermatologist, Dr. Chu, from the Abramson Cancer Center, Perleman School of Medicine at UPenn. Dr. Sargen from the Department of Dermatology at the Emory School of Medicine in Atlanta, Georgia, was also part of this case report that appeared in the *British Journal of Medicine*. The report was titled "CDKN2A Mutations with p14 Loss Predisposing to Multiple Nerve Sheath Tumors, Melanoma, Dysplastic Naevi and Internal Malignancies: A Case Series and Review of the Literature." I was very proud of my children for their decision to be part of this study, as it had the potential to not only help doctors, but other patients as well.

Something else happened during this time. I became a really good stair climber. I mean, really fast. I took all my anger out on the stairs.

And I was very, very angry. At the age of fifty I was winning races. Not merely winning my age group—I was the first female to reach the top. I was taking first overall in tower climbs all over the United States. I called this adversity training: I took a bad situation and pummeled it until it turned out positive.

Climbing 103 floors to the top of the Willis Tower (formerly the Sears Tower) in the SkyRise Chicago race. This was the tallest race until the Freedom Tower decided to start the runners a few floors underground to make the race 105 floors.

7

POLITICIANS, FIREFIGHTERS, AND ROCK STARS

TRAINING LOG
DATE: 1/13/2013
WORKOUT: 2.5 mile warm up; climbed 5 floors 10 times; sprinted 50 yards on roof and did 50 crunches and 10 push-ups at the top each time; 2.5 mile cool down
SPLITS: 22, 25, 27, 27, 26, 29, 26, 28, 27, 23

Stair climbing now occupied a very large box in my life. My three children were off at college, my job took no more than forty hours of my time each week, and my social life consisted of hanging out with other stair climbers, whether it was a workout in New York City or a post-race party. I became very close with some of my new friends, as we shared a special bond: participating in an extreme sport while raising funds for various charities. We referred to each other as "step-siblings." I was fortunate enough to become very good friends with two of the fastest male stair climbers in the United States, Stephen Marsalese and Jeff Gingold. We would often meet up for a stair workout, and they would push me beyond any limits I thought I had.

Unfortunately, as I became a better stair climber, I started to lose my biggest fan. My mother had attended all my track, cross country, and road races up through high school. She drove to some not-too-distant college events too. Later she cheered me on at some of the races I

I always have inspirational messages close by. My favorite is on the back of my phone.

trained a little harder for, including the New Jersey Marathon and two of the Timberbrook Triathlons. When she wasn't cheering me on, she attended almost every tennis match Paula and Dana ever had, and she watched Sam play in countless lacrosse and football games. She proudly volunteered every year at the Pine Beach 5K race when I was the race director. However, she never understood my stair climbing. She worried that it might be too strenuous for a woman in her fifties with a medical condition. But she accepted it—and even bragged about it. Even if she had wanted to cheer me on, she couldn't because stair climbs do not allow spectators in the stairwell, and very rarely do the races let anyone but the climbers and staff to be at the finish line on the top floor. Anyone not racing must wait in the lobby on the first floor. They can watch the runner start, enter the stairwell, and then wait to see that person again when they get off the elevator on the first floor—not too thrilling of a spectator sport. My biggest fan never even experienced that. She just got too sick and eventually succumbed to esophageal cancer on June 3, 2013.

On the day of my mother's service, it was the quintessential stormy funeral type of day: gray, windy, pouring rain, thunderstorms. You know, the type you see in a horror movie. Dana sheepishly came into my bedroom and very reluctantly said, "Mom, I hate to tell you this, but there is a leak in the roof, and water is coming into our bathroom." You know what? I didn't even care. I put a bucket on the floor to catch the water and finished getting ready. Shingles can be replaced. I could not replace the day I had to say goodbye to my biggest fan. Prioritizing is key, and perspective helps keep it all in order. Remember that the next time you need to put things in context.

A few months later I paid homage to my mother when I ran a Ragnar Relay. If she was alive at the time, I'm sure would have been very concerned yet proud that I was participating in a very grueling two hundred-mile race for the MMRF. I ran in her honor since the race started on her birthday in the foothills of western Maryland and finished in Washington, D.C., a place where my mother spent a lot of time as the New Jersey State Regent for the National Society of the Daughters of the American Revolution. By the way, I'm related to Charles the Great. My mother has our lineage going back to Charlemagne. Yup, I'm a princess.

TRAINING LOG
DATE: 3/22/2014
WORKOUT: 47 floors 6 times/NYC with Linda
TIME: 6:02, 6:33, 7:12, 6:58, 7:29, 6:10
NOTES: Great workout, bad day

Remember when I wrote that sometimes it seems as if bad times can last for years? Well, it seemed like my family was going through that when I missed a call from my sister while training in the city. My family was hit with our fourth death in our immediate family in just over four years. My nephew's sudden death was extremely tragic. We all wished we had noticed the warning signs to help prevent him from his permanent solution to a temporary situation when he committed suicide.

I have always believed that you have to dig deep inside of yourself to look for the good in each day, and that is what my sister did after she lost her son. She told me that I inspired her, but I admired her strength. Pat said she could let this ruin her or she could move on, and she choose the latter, although her laugh has never been the same since. Pat was always stronger and tougher than me. She inherited the most grit in the family. I have no doubt that if she had continued to race as long as me, she would have collected far more hardware than I.

If I can preach anything in this book, it is to heed the warning signs in order to prevent a crisis in your life, be it suicide, divorce, or whatever. Look, listen, and communicate. Communication is the key to *all* relationships, whether it's a friendship, a romantic relationship, or a work relationship. When it comes to work, you don't have to like your co-workers, but you must respect them. I'm not a relationship guru, but I was happily married for twenty years, and I learned that you need to communicate with your partner on every level to make the relationship work—and yes, it was hard work at times. But hard work pays off! I have never understood why some people work so hard on an affair. If they put that much time and energy into their marriage, it would probably be phenomenal.

Now that I'm on the topic of relationships, let me add that one of the problems with being a runner is that you must find someone who understands that you have to run, or at least exercise every day, and race on the weekends. Another quirk of being a runner is that you equate everything in your life with running, and that is exactly how I would describe my dating life at the age of fifty-two. I hadn't had a date in over thirty years, and I didn't know how or what I was doing. It seemed as though the rules changed from "going out" in the '70s and "hooking up" in the '80s. I had no idea if you were even supposed to kiss good night on the first date. Well, hell no, as far as I was concerned, if you weren't interested! And I was rarely interested. My daughter described me as a serial dater because the men that came along didn't have a long shelf life with me. I didn't need a man in my life to make me happy. Someone else can't make you happy. You make yourself happy.

However, like a race, I enjoyed dating. And like a race, I had the top three competing for the win. And what a prize I am!

During the race, I dated a politician through work who held the lead for quite a while, until I realized that I didn't enjoy politics 24/7, and therefore I didn't enjoy him that much either. I pretty much believe, "united we stand, divided we fall"—think about it: I couldn't date someone whose entire existence revolved around politics, and usually that is what happens with a politician. The parties were always the same: politicians pretending they are listening to you but really looking past you to make their next chess move. I felt like a pawn in the Big Boys Club. After he mentioned that "politicians eat their young," he was out, and second place moved quickly into first.

This competitor was a firefighter I met at a charity stair climb. I was impressed with his ability to climb entire buildings in full firefighter gear. Our long-distance relationship consisted of weekend rendezvous at various stair climbs around the country, where quite a few other women were also impressed with his stair climbing. Soon I saw a dark side of him. After a post-race party, he became very intoxicated and abusive, both verbally and physically. I saw firsthand that mental abuse can hurt just as much as physical abuse because it scars your mind. He was immediately disqualified from the race. No one would ever mentally control me. It was ironic that we both participated in a stair climb, Story by Story, where we raised money for Her Justice, an organization that assists low-income women with free legal help for many situations, including domestic violence. Unfortunately, some of these women cannot escape the violence because they are trapped, not financially stable enough or mentally strong enough to leave. I heard horrific stories of the evil preying upon these women. Obviously, I was not one of them. Luckily, I was able to read the warning signs with this guy, and I gracefully exited this destructive relationship unharmed. For anyone in an abusive relationship, man or woman (it can happen to both), your fight isn't over. You can leave. There is help. Contact Her Justice or other organizations. Be strong, practice grit, and believe in yourself. Never let anyone put you down to make themselves feel better. Steer clear of passive-aggressive people.

Third place was a long shot, a true wildcard. I don't even think he wanted to be in the race, let alone take the lead. He and I had known each other since kindergarten, but we hadn't seen each other since our senior year of high school. We reconnected the same way so many others in the digital age do—on Facebook. We found we had more in common than just our childhood. There was only one problem: He was now a rock star, and it's really, really difficult to date a rock star, especially when he is a world-renowned drummer and a very accomplished producer and musical director constantly touring around the world. At this time, he was playing with one of the highest-grossing tour artists of the year, Enrique Iglesias. Can you believe the Glen Ridge High School Class of 1980 produced such successful graduates? Along with this musician and Tom Cruise, there is also Brian Kelly, the chairman of Activison Blizzard, the fifth-largest gaming company in the world. We also had a professional tennis player, Ron Erskine, graduate with us! Not too shabby of alumni for a class of 205 students.

Back to the race . . . we tried to make our relationship work, but as it should be, his children were his top priority when he briefly stopped home between gigs. I had the utmost respect for his commitment to his family. Family is and should always be the largest box in your life. His career understandably required a huge box too. We realized we were better off as friends than lovers. We amicably agreed to end the romantic relationship but keep our friendship. Van Romaine is now one of my closet friends. Yes, men and women can be just friends. Again, communication is the key here. It's great to have a male friend I can call in the middle of the night and ask for some dating advice.

Three things I've learned from this race are:

1. You decide who gets a piece of your pie, and how big the piece will be.
2. Do not introduce your children to someone until you are absolutely sure they are the right person. They may be a good person, but that doesn't mean they are a good person for you.
3. Never ever go back and date an ex. They are an ex for a reason.

I know, you're reading this, sitting on the edge of your seat, biting your nails, and thinking, *OK, this may be good advice and all, but who won the race?* Sorry to disappoint you, but it was none of the above. Instead I was smitten by a faster, stronger, and very good-looking . . . *BuOY TOY. MY BuOY TOY*, to be exact. My new boat was exactly what I needed. Remember, you don't need another person to make you happy. And my boat has made me very happy. I feel alive and independent when I am with him. Yes, my boat is a male! I don't ride females.

This boat saved me. It literally was my rescue boat. For the first time in my life, I went boating alone. Growing up, I spent hours fishing with my father in his boat, *Putt Putt*. I'd sit in my puffy orange life jacket and rock back and forth in his little boat, bobbing like a floater in the bay, while my mom took my sisters to the beach. Later in life, Pete and I would take our children every weekend to the beach on the bay side of Island Beach State Park via our boat, *Sally's Spyder*.

Although I already had a boat, I wanted a new one—my very own boat. *Sally's Spyder* held some beautiful family memories of Pete and my children, but I needed a fresh start. I would keep the nostalgia, but I was ready to not live in the past. Personal growth requires shedding some of your past and starting new memories. That's why I sold *Sally's Spyder* and bought a nineteen-foot Century Bowrider with a four-stroke Yamaha 150 HP engine. This boat was tricked out. It boasted live wells for fishing, a freshwater hose, a GPS, a depth finder and a fish finder, rod holders, even a stereo and a marine radio. To top it all off, it had a ski pole so I could take Dana wakeboarding. I instantly fell in love with its navy blue hull and bright white interior. Even with all its amazing features, this boat was small enough for me to operate alone, but just big enough for me to cruise around the Toms River and Barnegat Bay, with an occasional trip out to the Atlantic Ocean on a calm day. I knew it was a great boat when I took it for a test drive with my brother-in-law Gary, and he said, "If you don't buy this boat, then I will." With my sister Sue and Gary's help, we took the maiden voyage and docked *MY BuOY TOY* at Shore Point Marina, which was located just a mile and a half down the road from my house. I admired their nonchalant attitude that day when their new car was hit at the marina while helping me. They, too, knew there were more important things in life to worry about.

Despite the accident at the marina, I loved the place. Shore Point Marina became my home away from home. There I met a new group of friends, my dock buddies. However, I started to spend a little bit more time with one particular boater. We spent countless hours on the water getting to know one another before our relationship got deeper, just like the waters we navigated together. (Boy, that sounded deep— no pun intended. Actually, we just got to know each other really well before we started to date.) Sometimes I'd go to the marina to get away from everyone and everything, and other times I'd hang out with my new friends or entertain old ones and family on my boat. Mostly, I loved taking *MY BuOY TOY* out by myself. I loved the challenge of operating a vessel on my own. Like life, no two days on the water are ever the same. Mastering the challenge of the ever-changing winds, tides, and current were very rewarding. I was finally free. I found happiness again. I gave *MY BuOY TOY* a huge box in my life—a box that had been empty for a long time.

Finally it seemed as if everything was going well. I felt that I had finally struck the perfect balance in my life. Once I took the boat out of the water for the winter, I'd start training hard again in New York City and travel to races all over North America, including Canada, on the weekends. Once the stair climbing season came to an end in late spring, I'd put the boat back in the water and give my body a break. I'd cross-train with less stair climbing and some running, along with some kayaking and biking. Besides, I did not want to spend a beautiful, warm day in a hot, stuffy stairwell when I lived at the shore. This is a perfect example of how I would expand and shrink the boxes in my life.

You would never know I was doing all of this with a small hole in my hip, called a lytic lesion. The multiple myeloma had started to eat away at my bone, the second place multiple myeloma likes to invade after the bloodstream and before an organ. There comes a time in almost every cancer patient's life when they are given the choice of quality of life or quantity of life. Well, me being the youngest and therefore the most spoiled, I wanted both. The treatment to fill the hole in my bone had the potential for a very bizarre side effect in women: It could cause an enlarged jaw bone. *Hmm,* I thought, *a tiny hole in my hip that I can't see and barely feel, or a Dudley Do Right chin?* Being somewhat vain, I chose to deal with the minor pain. My doctor agreed with my decision since the hole was very small, and he would now monitor me even more closely for any more progression of multiple myeloma.

TRAINING LOG
DATE: 8/15/15
WORKOUT: Bike and Bar with Jo: biked 15 miles and hit 4 bars along the way back

When I was in Chicago to race up Willis (formerly the Sears Tower)—which, at 103 floors, happened to be the tallest stair climb race in America at the time—I met the president of the Tower World Association, Michael Reichetzeder. At the pre-climb social for elite racers, he told me I was ranked in the top fifty women in the world. Surprised, I asked, "Top fifty in my age group?" He replied in his thick Austrian accent, "No, top fifty women overall in the world." Yikes! I knew I was one of the top women in the States according to Tower

Running USA, but I never bothered to look at the world standings. I never imagined I'd be one of the top stair climbers in the world. Well, that was all I needed to hear to start training like a maniac. Not just any maniac—a full-fledged, two to three workouts-per-day maniac. I wanted to see how much better I could get.

A few months later I traveled to Las Vegas to compete in the USA National Stair Climbing Championships. There I met another person that would inspire me to step outside of my comfort zone and set new goals in my life. Stepsister Jane Trahanovsky is the author of *See Jane Climb*. *Drats,* I thought to myself, *what a great name for a book! Why didn't I think of that?* Well, not Jane, but Sally. *See Sally Climb* would have been perfect. I confessed to Jane that I loved to write, but never had the guts to share any of it. She convinced me to let her read some of my work, which I reluctantly did. For the first time in my life, I let someone read some of my writing. Jane was so impressed with my work that she put me in contact with her editor and publisher. I submitted some excerpts from three different manuscripts. The first was my favorite, a fictional story that I thought was funny, the second was a children's book that I thought was educational, and the third was my least favorite, my memoirs that I thought were boring. It figures; they chose my memoirs. I really didn't want to write about myself. I knew that I might have inspired a few people, but I didn't think my story was *that* compelling.

I got very lucky that weekend in Vegas. Not only was I the ninth female overall to get to the top of the Stratosphere, but I also scored big by meeting Jane, which led me to signing a contract for my book. In fact, someone told me I was dealt a bad hand. I laughed as I replied, "Are you kidding me? I'm making the best of the cards I was given and having fun playing. I'm winning."

That year I did my fifth and fastest ESBRU to date. My time of 18:01 placed me as the eighteenth overall female, and helped my world ranking. In April 2016, Tower World Association ranked me as the twentieth overall female tower runner in the world and fifth in the United States. I was invited to participate in the third edition of the La Verticale de la Tour Eiffel on March 17, 2017, a race up the 1,665 stairs to the top of the Eiffel Tower!

			TWA Ranking Females April 2016			Score	Dev.	All Races Races	Tour	Total
1	1	0	Lenka Svabikova	CZE		908.5	22.0	9	6	15
3	2	1	Dominika Wisniewska-Ulfik	POL		861.0	120.0	3	6	9
2	3	-1	Suzanne Walsham	AUS		860.0	0.0			
6	4	6	Cindy Harris	USA		574.0	120.0	5	4	9
5	5	0	Cristina Bonacina	ITA		567.0	0.0	4	4	8
4	6	0	Zuzana Krchova	CZE		541.0	0.0	6	8	14
7	7	-3	Iwona Wicha	POL		538.0	-60.0	1	4	5
8	8	0	Stephanie Hucko	USA		510.0	0.0	4	2	6
9	9	0	Jasmina Klancnik	SLO		507.5	2.0	3	4	7
10	10	-3	Veronica Stocker	CAN		436.0	-102.0	12	4	16
11	11	0	Cindy Reid	AUS		429.0	0.0	5	2	7
12	12	0	Fengjuan Fan	CHN		384.0	0.0	7	1	8
13	13	1	Maike Grossmann	GER		367.5	46.0	5	1	6
14	14	-1	Sylvia Jacobs	GER		331.0	6.0	5	4	9
15	15	0	Lisa Zeigel	USA		322.0	10.0	3	2	5
17	16	0	Brooke Logan	AUS		310.0	0.0	8	4	12
16	17	0	Xue Gan	CHN		290.0	0.0	2	3	5
18	18	0	Linda Viner	USA		269.0	0.0	3	0	3
20	19	0	Anna Ficner	POL		268.0	0.0	4	3	7
21	20	8	Sally Kalkama	USA		241.0	66.0	1	1	2
14	21	1	Christine Soskins	USA		234.0	-2.0	7	2	9
22	22	1	Veronika Sengstbrati	AUT		227.5	0.0	3	2	5
24	23	4	Egle Uljas	EST		224.0	26.0	5	1	6
25	24	-3	Sabine Nader	AUT		222.5	-20.0	1	4	5
26	25	0	Maria Eugenia Rodriguez	COL		210.0	0.0	4	2	6
27	26	-2	Kamila Chomanicova	SVK		206.0	-6.0	8	2	4

Tower World Association rankings for April 2016 when I was ranked 20th overall female in the world, and 5th overall female in the USA.

8

A NEW BIRTHDAY

TRAINING LOG
DATE: 5-15-16
LOCATION: 4 World Trade Center
WORKOUT: 78 floors – 4 times
TIME: 15:58, 16:22, 17:01, 16:36
NOTES: Last hard workout before Freedom Tower

Dr. S always warned me I would need treatment when my immunoglobulin G (IgG) hit a "magic number." Measuring IgG, which is a type of antibody, and about fifty other things in the blood is some magical, mystical way that doctors can figure out how much multiple myeloma is in your body. They take about twelve vials of blood each time. I was never too concerned with this magic number because every time my number would rise a bit, it would somehow drop back down at the next checkup three months later. I took excellent care of myself, despite beating my body up a bit on the stairs. I watched everything I ate and drank, and I gave my body a lot of rest to recuperate. Dr. S pointed out that this past year my numbers were peaking a little higher and not dropping as far back down as they had in the past, and so he wanted to see me again in another month. Sure enough, I hit that magic number at my next checkup. Dr. S said I needed to start treatment. I asked him when, and he replied, "Now." It was a shock to hear since I was racing the best I ever had in my entire life. At the age of fifty-four, I felt that I was in the greatest shape of my life. Well, being in such good shape going into treatment was a blessing. My body was ready to take on its biggest challenge to date.

The first thing I had to do was have another dreaded bone marrow biopsy to determine exactly how much multiple myeloma was in my body before starting chemotherapy. I was stunned with the results. I couldn't believe the cancer was aggressive enough to be in half of my blood. Wow! Now that we had our answer, I would start treatment. I say "we" because I had a healthcare team working with me: the receptionist, the nurses, the healthcare coordinator, and my two oncologists. I had two oncologists because Dr. S. advised me to also have a local oncologist, a specialist closer to home so I wouldn't have to drive two hours in case complications from chemo were to arise, which was common. Dr. S was and still is my primary oncologist, and Dr. Sara McGee would assist.

I also had a strong support group made up of family, friends, and my Cancer Care Buddy, or CCB. My best friend, Linda, was my CCB. She went above and beyond the call of a best friend. She accompanied me on all of my checkups and treatments. This was not a convenient task for her because she lived and worked in Manhattan. She selflessly took days off from work, drove to my house in Pine Beach, New Jersey, and then drove me, not only to the doctor in neighboring Toms River, but also the two additional hours to Philadelphia. As if navigating the ninety minutes of New York City traffic to the Jersey Shore wasn't enough, she was willing to throw in another major metropolitan city's worth of congestion. When I was admitted into the hospital, she would stay at a nearby hotel. Her background in pharmaceutical marketing was a huge asset when deciphering medical lingo. In true best-friend fashion, we had a lot of laughs, and a lot of very good meals along the way to and from UPenn. Linda and I became closer, as I did with my entire team.

It is so important to have a close relationship with your team because they are all working to keep you, the patient, alive. Everyone plays an important role in your health.

There are not too many options for treatment of multiple myeloma. Blood cancers are unlike other cancers. Doctors cannot cut out a tumor and then radiate the area because at stage one multiple myeloma is in your stem cells, which run throughout your entire body. Therefore, the doctor must use a lot of drugs to eliminate the bad cells in your body. Of course, the treatment kills a lot of good cells at the same time, causing increased fatigue, weakness, and a low immune system, along with the usual stomach issues that I promise you do not want to read about. One of the things I learned to do by having multiple myeloma is to accept pain. Not only do you have to learn to deal with it, but in a twisted, crazy, masochistic way, you have to like it if it is the result of the treatment. You must understand that it is one of the steps toward getting healthy, similar to a workout: it will hurt, but it is making you stronger, faster, and better.

I was hoping to be accepted into a clinical trial that potentially would not have the same nasty side effects as the treatment I was about to begin. Unfortunately, the clinical trial began before I could enter. Therefore, I started with the widely used Revilimad/Velcade/ Dexamethasone (RVD). This treatment had a good success rate. How could it not? Not only are you ingesting chemo (Revlimad) every day, but they are also injecting chemo (Velcade) into your body once a week, as well as giving you heavy doses of steroids (Dexamethasone, or just Dex) to combat the side effects of the chemo. However, the steroids caused some pretty bad side effects too. Out of all the drugs that were pumped into my body, the steroids were my least favorite, or maybe I should say, the most dreaded. The chemo messed with my body, but the steroids messed with my brain. And I was given a lot more than just these three drugs. When I felt bad, I had to keep telling myself it was the drugs, not me.

The RVD treatment was to last six months. Of course, all the boxes in my life had to shift. Treatment consumed a good portion of my time, and the side effects chipped away at some valuable time too. I had to prioritize. My number one priority was to make the best of the situation I was in, since it was the only situation I could be in at this time in my life. I actually looked forward to going to the doctor for my weekly shots of Velcade. Obviously, I didn't look forward to my weekly bloodwork, followed by the needle in my stomach, and then the feeling of the cool burn of chemo running through my veins. But I did look forward to spending time with Linda. And we both looked forward to seeing the nurse with the great sense of humor, Anthony. He administered the chemo. We all joked that he and the chemo were both my friend and foe.

Laughter truly is one of the best medicines. Nothing makes me feel better than laughing, and I can find humor in a lot of things, bad and good. When Dr. S told me I would be admitted into the hospital for a couple of days for a strong intravenous dose of chemo called Cytoxan (it even sounds potent with the word *toxin* in it), they put me in a beautiful room in the Rhoades wing. I thought to myself, *Wow, I must really be sick if they're putting me in a room that looks like this.* The view of the Ivy League school was right out of a movie. My sister Marion remarked that my room looked like a resort. She called it the "Rhoades Resort at UPenn." Once settled in, Dr. S broke the ice to me when he half-jokingly said, "You have really nice hair; it's a shame you're going to lose it." Well, you know what I did? As soon as I was discharged from the hospital, I immediately went out and bought ten different wigs so I could be a different woman every day: Roxy, Mercedes, Bobby Jo, Natasha, Xavier—you get the picture, right? Well, here's the buzz kill. I'm sorry to ruin your fantasy, but I never wore one wig, not even once. I soon found out that I had a pretty decent-shaped head.

After the Cytoxan was slowly dripped into my veins, Dr. S made his rounds. Our conversation was nothing like all my other checkups where he would ask how I was doing, and I would boast about all my races. This time when he asked the same question, I replied, "I think I'm about to get sick." With that answer, I ran to the bathroom and vomited. When I returned, he said, "Yes, my medicine's working. If that didn't happen, I wouldn't be doing my job. I finally got to you; I knocked you down." That is what the chemo does, it knocks you down. It is not what I allowed the cancer to do.

This heavy dose of chemo was just another one of the prerequisites before an autologous stem cell transplant (SCT). There is a misunderstanding that a SCT helps eliminate the cancer. Not true. A SCT is to help keep the patient in remission longer. The doctors cannot put healthy cells in your body if there are still bad ones because the bad ones will just eat up the good ones. The patient, me in this case, has to be cancer-free before a SCT. Therefore, the doctors had to bomb me with an even heavier dose of chemo before my upcoming SCT. But not just yet—the doctors still had more voodoo to perform on me.

My white count started to bottom out a few days after I was released from the hospital (a side effect of the heavy chemo). I became very weak. My red cells and plasma started to drop, while the pain increased. Everything started to hurt. One night I collided with Blue Dog. I fell to the floor in pain. I told Paula that all my bones just broke. They didn't, but I did develop bruises all over my body. My blood could not clot, which was another one of the side effects of the heavy chemo. To boost my white

My healthcare team at the University of Pennsylvania Hospital gave me this calendar of events that I needed to follow leading up to my stem cell transplant.

count, I had to administer shots of Neupogen in my stomach via a needle every night for two weeks. My good friend Tamila Purporo, a nurse, came to my house and taught me how to poke myself since I didn't quite understand the directions that were given to me in the large white binder that also housed my schedule of lab appointments, medicines, and procedures.

TRAINING LOG
DATE: 1/22/17
LOCATION: Homewood Suites, Philadelphia
WORKOUT: 11 floors 10 times, 300 crunches, 100 pushups

The next step a real-life voodoo doll does prior to an autologous SCT is to go back to the hospital as an outpatient to harvest the cells the doctors would use for the transplant. This process takes anywhere from one to five days. Since no one knows exactly how long it will take for someone's body to extract 9 million white blood cells, another close friend, Wendy Mele, arranged for me to stay in a nearby hotel. She did this so I wouldn't have to do the daily four-hour round trip. Wendy is not only the sweetest person you will ever meet, she is also one of the most exciting and eccentric. Her heart is so big. When I told her that summer that I started chemo, she whisked me away to the Ocean Place Resort and Spa in Long Branch, New Jersey, for a weekend of pampering. I teased her husband, Dennis, that my cancer was costing him a lot of money.

During the stem cell harvest, I spent my days hooked up to a large apparatus that sounded like an old washing machine with a load of spinning, lopsided towels and looked like something from the 1960 television show, *Lost in Space*. Wendy would gallivant around Philly, exploring art museums and unique shops. At night, we would have dinner delivered to our suite and watch old movies. We did this while I looked like a sci-fi creature with two tubes dangling out of my neck. One tube took all my blood out and put it into the machine that separated the white, the plasma, and the red cells. It kept the white cells and the plasma for my transplant, and then it put the red cells back into the machine to be warmed up and put back into my body via the other tube. I was hooked up to this machine for four hours every day until enough cells were collected for three transplants. Some people are lucky enough to get a collection in one or two days, while others take up to a week. My body was one of the stingy ones that took five days. Patients who are going to have an allogenic stem cell transplant (as opposed to an autologous one) do not harvest their cells because they receive their cells from another person. The donor must be a 100-percent match to avoid graft-versus-host disease, which can be fatal. Dr. S said I would have to have an allogenic stem cell transplant if the autologous transplant did not work.

That was the week I started to lose my hair. It came out in clumps. I didn't want to be rude because I was sharing the bathroom with Wendy, so I made an appointment with the UPenn hairdresser. (Yeah, there is such a person. The hospital actually has a hair salon that even makes "room" calls.) During my appointment, the hairstylist would take a little off at a time and then stop and ask if I wanted to go shorter. It was a no brainer to shave it all off so I wouldn't keep shedding. At first, every time I looked in a mirror, I was like "Whoa, is that me?" Although my head was so cold, I quickly warmed up to my new look. When my sister Marion asked what I needed before coming to visit me, I told her hats. I needed a real sleeping cap at night. However, the mornings were great because I could get ready in a flash. The first time I took a shower with no hair, I just stood there and said to myself, "Okay, now what do I do?" What I did was spend more time on applying a lot of makeup, and I wore different beaded headpieces. I loved being bald. When else can you be a full-fledged diva?

Believe it or not, it was a fun week. Not only did I enjoy my time with Wendy, but I looked forward to seeing the flirtatious hotel shuttle driver, Wayne, who drove me to and from the hospital each day. I had a lot of laughs with the young intern who was attending medical school at UPenn. We shared so many bad jokes that one time I laughed so hard that I blew the bandages off my neck. Blood went everywhere since I couldn't clot. He frantically tried to stop the bleeding while I tried to stop laughing. It literally was a bloody mess.

After my stem cell harvest, I went home to recoup for a few days before heading back to the hospital for my transplant. I was very fortunate to have Paula stay with me during treatment. Not only did she take care of me and put up with my raging steroid fits, but she also took care of the dogs and the house. She did all this while working full-time with a long commute to Rowan University (formerly Glassboro State College, my alma mater) where she taught.

My game face as I took on multiple myeloma.

After six months of treatment, I finally made it to the last and most important step: the stem cell transplant. On January 31, 2017, I woke up early to enjoy time with Paula, my house, and my dogs before leaving for an unknown period of time. Again I was put in a room by myself. My isolation room would be my home away from home for a minimum of three weeks. This day was called Day Minus Two. In two days, I would have my SCT—Tuesday, February 2nd, 10:30 a.m., to be exact. The expansive and expensive medical team start the count from the day you are admitted into the hospital and they administer the super strong chemo Melphalan. The day of my transplant would be considered Day Zero. February 3rd would be Day Plus One, and so on. February 2nd would be my new birthday. Just like the movie *Groundhog Day*, I was starting the same life all over again, but this time healthier.

Day Minus Two was very busy. After seeing the doctor, I was sent to have my PICC line inserted, a 48-centimeter line placed in my forearm that ran to my chest. This would be my lifeline for all of my meds, labs, and most importantly, cells. I was finally settled in my room by 3:00 p.m. Let me change the word *settled* to just *in*, as I was never really ever settled. I was trying my best to control my nerves. I spent the next few hours trying to stay upbeat while I unpacked and met with many of the people on my care team. Two became my favorites: Nurse Ellen and Nurse Matt. Although Matt was an Eagles fan, I told him we'd still be friends. At 8:15 p.m., I was finally given the Melphalan. This chemo medication is so strong that it practically brings you down to death's door. Every count in my body would eventually drop to almost zero, even though the drip took only twenty minutes. All evening they kept giving me fluids, meds, and IV drips. I was exhausted.

TRAINING LOG
DATE: February 1, 2017
WORKOUT: 20 minutes of walking & lunges/Biked 10 minutes
NOTES: Very dehydrated; Needed a lot of extra fluids.

Surprisingly, even with lines hooked up to my arm, I slept great. As the staff predicted, Day Minus One was a good day. The nausea had not yet kicked in, nor had my counts begun to drop. I felt like I was on my way back to normal. This was my rest day, and it went well. Although I didn't have any visitors, I actually preferred it that way. I got a lot of alone time in, and I got to know the great staff. And I was determined to get some exercise in. During my twenty-minute workout, I noticed an exercise bike in the hall. The physical therapist happened to be on the floor and noticed me doing lunges. When I finished, she came in my room, evaluated me, and gave me that bike. However, I wasn't allowed to use the exercise bands I packed. The PT said they could get tangled in my PICC lines. The nurses also informed me I was not allowed to do any weight-bearing exercises while my platelet count was so low.

Most of the day my mind was consumed with the ESBRU. That night was the race. This would be the first time I missed it in six years. Ironically, what brought me to stair climbing was now taking it away, at least temporarily. I was so excited for all of my step-sibs. But I was especially excited for Dana, as she took my spot in the race. Like me, after she did her first ESBRU, she said she would never do it again. And there she was, doing it again, this time for me and the MMRF. She did an amazing job of fundraising and competing. She made me very proud and psyched to go into my SCT the next day. Dana climbed what I feel is the hardest building in the world in 17:52, was the thirteenth overall female finisher, was second in the 20–29 age group, and won the coveted first female overall for the MMRF—something I had always wanted but had yet to achieve. Now it no longer mattered. Dana got it! After the race Dana confessed that she hated every single step, but she loves me, so she did it. I was very lucky to have the love and support of my family, friends, step-siblings, and MMRF. I felt I was 100 percent ready for my SCT.

After a sleepless night filled with anticipation, excitement, and the effects of Dex, which doesn't let you sleep, Day Zero arrived! I got out of bed at 6:00 a.m. so I could grab some coffee from the pantry down the hall and hop in the shower before they connected me to my fluid drip at 6:30 a.m. Once I was hooked back up, I went for a twenty-minute walk around the hall with my rolling infusion pump stand, named Wilson after the beloved volleyball Tom Hanks befriends in *Castaway*. Wilson stayed by my side the entire time I was in the hospital—not that he had a choice.

That day breakfast was running late. My SCT was scheduled for 10:30 a.m. The team started to assemble at 9:45. My breakfast arrived at 9:35, and to make matters worse, it was not what I ordered. I think this small fiasco helped contribute to the nausea I had later. Marion and Linda arrived right after breakfast. Marion was my photographer, and the doctor had no problem posing for her. My cells arrived in a large rolling metal container that looked like an oven with pots on top. The doctor would remove each of the four frozen bags I was to receive only when the prior bag was done being dripped into my body.

It was a fascinating process to watch. I was hooked up to a heart rate monitor and several other monitors that two nurses and an assistant constantly watched. The doctor would remove a bag, defrost it to body temperature, then hand it to the nurse practitioner, who would then attach a pump to the bag and attach the bag to my PICC line. She would then pump in the cells. Each bag took approximately five minutes. The whole procedure took less than thirty minutes. During that half hour, I had to constantly chew on ice for some odd reason.

The atmosphere was very upbeat; we all introduced ourselves, and of course, I made some of my stupid jokes. The nurse practitioner was from Germany, which we found out after Marion told them about her sixtieth German birthday party. That led to us telling them that we liked to have a party for everything. I told them about the "chemo kick-off party" I hosted when I started treatment the previous summer. My sister and I explained that we inherited our love for throwing parties from our mother, who even threw her own "Last Rites" party from her hospital bed. My entire family was present when the priest came in her living room. My mom even treated everyone to a delicious meal catered from the infamous Joe Leone's in Point Pleasant.

Today, Marion, Linda and I would have a SCT party. The SCT was not as difficult as you might imagine—I really only felt discomfort when they started to pump the fourth bag into my line. My chest got very tight and my oxygen level went from 100 to 94. They adjusted some things and I felt better, except for an odd feeling in my throat.

As soon as the SCT was over, the doctor and the nurse practitioner said goodbye, wheeled the medicine out of the room, and disappeared, like a magician and his assistant with their magic box. By the time the rest of my nurses left the room, I felt like nothing had happened. Marion, Linda, and I resumed our party. I posed for photos with hair, saying that the SCT worked so well that my hair immediately grew back. However, later in the day, I began to get tired and felt very nauseous. That night I could not even look at my dinner. I drank two small cartons of chocolate milk. During my birthday celebration, I went from Mustang Sally to Groundhog Sally.

On Day Plus One the nausea and tiredness continued—an accumulation of everything my body had gone through coupled with the chemo. I was hoping I would have a few more days of somewhat normalcy, but no such luck. I felt lousy. The only saving grace that day was when my daughters came to visit. Paula told me she was meeting a friend for lunch, but what she really did was cut off all her beautiful, long, curly locks, and donate them to cancer patients. She looked more beautiful than ever when she walked in my room with her chic new bob.

Dana took the bus from New York City and then walked almost a mile to the hospital with all of her weekend bags. She pulled out a gift for me: her first-place crystal trophy from the ESBRU and her bib number. Yes, I got all choked up. The girls spent the afternoon catching up, and I just listened. After Paula left, Linda stopped in. I was hoping not to disappoint her too much when I told her I was too tired to build the LEGO Eiffel Tower that my friend Lee gave me. The three of us just watched *Family Feud*. Linda left at 9:00 p.m., and at 10:00 p.m. Dana went downstairs to wait for her boyfriend Derek. The sleeping pills had me crash as soon as Dana left the room.

All my blood counts started to decline on Day Plus Two. The nurses hung a "Daily Blood Count Record" chart on my bulletin board alongside my "Get Well Cards" and photos of my family and friends. This chart kept track of my WBC (white blood count), ANC (absolute neutrophil count, a type of white cells that fight infection), HgB (hemoglobin count, which is the measurement of red blood cells), and PLT (platelets, the blood cells that help the body form clots to stop bleeding). It also listed the day of my SCT and the four subsequent times I would need blood and platelet transfusions. It was unimaginable that some of my numbers hit zero. I was not allowed to be released from the hospital until they were close to normal, although I wouldn't be totally recovered for months. I was amazed at how low my numbers dropped and looked forward to watching them rise up again. When my numbers were at rock bottom, I didn't have an immune system. My visitors had to be healthy, and they had to wear masks. My visitors on Day Plus Two were Dana and Derek. They spent most of the day with me, chatting and coloring in some of the many coloring books I received. The highlight of my day was when they brought me a mint chocolate chip milkshake.

Day Plus Three was big. I had two things to look forward to. I remembered to sign up for the Spring Lake Five when my labs were drawn at 5:00 a.m. I was so psyched, not only because I had something to work for, but because this five mile race is the largest in the country and sells out in hours once registration opens at the crack of dawn. My goal was to finish, be it walk or run, five miles by May 27. Afterward I could see all my friends at Bar A. After I signed up for the race, I immediately texted my family and friends to remind them to do the same! Later that day two of my running friends and a Tower Master teammate came to visit. However, the nurses did not allow them to stay long because I needed to nap. I wanted to be well rested for the Super Bowl Party that I was hosting that evening. What better place than my increasingly lonely room to have a party? Since technically I was in isolation, I had a large private room, with my own bathroom, and my own mini fridge. The long ledge along the windowsill was perfect for the buffet. Being the ever-perfect hostess, my refrigerator was already stocked with beer for my visitors. For anyone who preferred a cocktail, I had some hard alcohol that I snuck into the hospital in my suitcase. I hid it in the back of my closet behind my robe. I also had plenty of mixers. There was ginger ale, orange juice, cranberry juice, and for those crazy enough, Ensure, all "borrowed" from the community kitchen on my floor. The only thing I lacked was food—or at least *good* food. I wouldn't dare subject my guests to saltines and leftover hospital food! My sister Jo and her husband Dennis brought the wings and subs. Paula and her boyfriend (now husband) Rob brought some chips and dip. There was a wonderful turnout of friends and family. Even the hospital staff checked on me a little more than usual that night, and not because they were worried about my health.

Day Plus Five was probably the lowest I have ever felt in my entire life, both mentally and physically. My counts were so low that I couldn't do anything. I couldn't even get out of bed. When I tried, I literally fell on the floor, which immediately branded me. The nurse put caution tape on my door, along with a sign that said "FALL RISK." She also added another rubber identification bracelet to my wrist that said the same thing in bright yellow. How humiliating! One of the best tower runners in the world, and now I'm a fall risk! It was funny to think I used to wear rubber bracelets after a race to get a free beer.

By Day Plus Six, I looked and felt like a zombie in a B movie horror film. When I was admitted into the hospital on the "liquid floor," a term they use for blood cancer patients, I saw sick-looking warriors battling their cancer as they shuffled around in their pajamas. I said I would never be one of those people. Well, it didn't take me long to become one. On this day I walked very, very slowly around the halls—with a hole in my pajama bottoms, on the butt no less. I didn't even care that Paula mistakenly brought me the wrong pajama bottoms when we exchanged my laundry. I was too focused on using every bit of energy I had to do two laps around the nurse's station. I didn't want to be like the frail young man in the room next to mine. He told me that he came from the Midwest and had been at UPenn since Thanksgiving. There was nothing left for the doctors to do for him, so he planned on leaving as soon as his parents could get enough money to try an experimental drug overseas. This wasn't a bad movie. It was real life.

I hit my lowest point on Day Plus Nine. My absolute neutrophil count hit zero; my platelets and white and red blood cells were almost as low. My poor visitors that day witnessed my body go into shock. They sat and watched the first of two emergency blood transfusions. The second blood transfusion was given the next day before a platelet transfusion.

I didn't have any brain cells left at this point, not that I had many to begin with. Fortunately, I enjoy writing, and I kept journals about my stay. If I hadn't kept these journals, I wouldn't remember a majority of what happened to me. The hallucinations from the chemo did not help my situation either. One night I just sat in bed and watched the walls turn different shades of purple. As the days went on, I wrote less and less in my journal. It's not that I didn't want to; I simply couldn't. It became too hard for me to think clearly, and it definitely was too difficult for me to write. Thanks goodness I kept a guest book. I asked everyone who came to visit me to sign in. I still love to look back and read all the encouraging messages.

This is the chart of my daily blood counts that hung on the bulletin board in my hospital room. You can see that I dropped to zero. I couldn't be discharged until my counts were close to normal.

I was so blessed to have visitors every day except for that one day, and

I was pleasantly surprised at who made the trek from various places. I was also disappointed at who didn't. I remembered Pete once saying, "You find out who your true friends are by who comes to visit you in the hospital." It was hard not to feel let down. I tried to remind myself that everyone has something going on in their lives, too, but the same stages of grief I went through when Pete passed were reemerging again: remorse, anger at everyone and everything, and betrayal. Only this time I did not have the energy to take my negative feelings out on a workout. I had to work these feelings out in my head.

I was also mad at the multiple myeloma patients who were still in the smoldering stage yet complaining of their diagnosis. To me, these patients hadn't gone through the treatment, the same rites of passage we did, the patients whose cancer progressed into full-blown multiple myeloma. I felt even more disdain toward cancer-free people who had no idea what it was like to be a patient. And don't tell me about being a caregiver. It's not the same. I've been there. Linda told me not to expect anything from anyone so I wouldn't be disappointed. She was right.

To keep an upbeat outlook, I had to remember what I told myself before treatment: I wanted to be a better person when it was all over. I told the cancer, "I have you; you don't have me. Nor will you ever. Although you are trying to get the best of me, there is no doubt that I will win. I will do everything possible, physically and mentally, to annihilate you, destroy you, and kill you. And when I'm done, I will help other cancer warriors fight too." I kept looking for the positives while in the hospital. Valentine's Day was positive, for example. I didn't have to deal with the snow that accumulated overnight, and Paula and her friend Jordan came to visit me. They decorated my room with balloons and brought me lots of candy, which I shared with the nurses. When they left, my favorite cousin, Keith, stopped by. After dinner, I attended an ice cream social on my floor, where The HEADstrong Foundation treated all the cancer patients at UPenn to ice cream and board games. This foundation was founded by a patient, Nick

Colleluori, whose last wish was to help families affected by cancer by offering financial, residential, and emotional support. Now that was really positive!

To keep the positivity going, I was lucky enough to get discharged from the hospital after seventeen days! On the last day, I woke up before dawn, showered, dressed, and packed up. Marion and her husband, Rick, who were driving me home, arrived early because they knew I couldn't wait to leave. Of course, it took hours for everything to be just right, between all the instructions and medicines I was given to go home with. They even gave me a platelet transfusion before I left. When it was finally time to leave, Dr. S said I did so well and responded beautifully to treatment because I went into this in such good shape.

9

THE IRON LADY

TRAINING LOG
DATE: March 2, 2017
WORKOUT: Walked two blocks to Pocket Park with Pat
NOTES: Exhausted

Once again, my house was transformed into a "hospital ward." The dining room became my exam room. The marble dining table housed all my medical supplies and medications.

Twice weekly the nurse would stop by to take my vitals and change the dressing on the PICC line that that had been inserted over a month ago. My sister Pat came up from Tennessee to help me while I was recuperating. When she suggested this, I didn't think I would need her. I was so wrong. I needed someone with me while Paula was at work. There was no way I could cook or clean up after myself. It took all my energy to walk down the stairs, and even then, I was totally drained. I spent hours just staring out the window. My brain was shot. This worried Pat because she said I reminded her of our mom when she was dying. It was a very humbling experience. I realized you should never be too proud to accept help when you really need it. Maybe the other person needs to help you more than you need them. However, as I found out, this time that wasn't the case with me.

It was insane that I couldn't even walk fifty yards without stopping to rest. Each day I tried to walk a little farther with Pat as she walked my dogs. Sometimes I would stop and sit at a park bench, but not for too long. My godmother, Aunt Pip, said, "If you rest, you rust."

My sister Sue came over for a few days to give Pat a break. It was a little out of their comfort zone preparing my neutropenic meals. When your white blood cell counts are super low like mine were, you are not allowed to eat most fresh fruits or vegetables because your body simply doesn't have what it takes to fight off any organisms that may be living on them and could make you very sick. An orange or a banana was fine because I could peel off the skin. Any food like berries or broccoli were forbidden, even if it was cleaned and cooked. Nor was I allowed any type of deli meat, cheeses, nuts, or grains. Meat could only be consumed if it was very well done. This was difficult for everyone in the house, as they all liked to cook, and the neutropenic diet just did not leave room for any creativity or favorite dishes. I craved for Pat's famous Pizza Bread. Even fresh flowers and plants were not allowed in the house. As soon as the doctors said it was okay for me to drink alcohol again, I too, planned to cook—well, sort of. I planned to make a batch of my homemade limoncello to give out as a thank you to those who were there for me during this difficult time. Some people make lemonade out of lemons—I like to go the extra step and make "Smilin' Sal's Homemade Limoncello."

A bottle of my "Smilin' Sal's Homemade Limoncello."

It took several weeks for me to get some of my strength back, but I was still nowhere near 100 percent yet. Gradually I was able to take care of myself. However, I dreaded the day that Pat's husband, Bob, was coming to pick her up. I loved the company since I wasn't allowed to go out in public yet. When I did venture out, it was to go for a slow run with Paula. Our workouts were a stark difference from the days when she was a small child accompanying me on a run. Back then she would ask me to slow down. Now I was begging her to reduce the pace. There was no physical way I could have competed in the race up the Eiffel Tower on March 16, 2017. Thankfully, the committee was kind enough to defer me until 2018. I had another goal!

Dr. S told me I could return to work in May. However, I had one important thing to do before that. I flew down to my favorite city in the United States, Charleston, South Carolina, to visit Sam and his girlfriend (now fiancée), Allison. This quick jaunt was a much-needed respite. During that time, I did a stair workout in my hotel and ran on the beach. I was back, or so I thought.

Now that I had regained some of my strength, Dr. S put me back on chemo, but this time as maintenance therapy. Every night I had to take Revlimad. Along with the chemo came a new side effect that would haunt me to this day: neuropathy. The Velcade I took before my SCT had caused a delayed debilitating pain that had an oxymoron of side effects. On one end of the spectrum I did not have any feelings in my hands and feet during the day. At night when I tried to sleep, I felt like someone had set my feet on fire and then proceeded to hit them repeatedly with a sledgehammer. Over the next three years, I had six episodes where the neuropathy caused me to break two bones, tear four ligaments, and dislocate one joint, none of which I felt happening at the time.

Neuropathy gave a whole new meaning to a phrase we often used in high school: "No pain, no gain." Now I had no pain, and it was hard for me to gain. In high school, there was a lot of pain, and a lot of gains, which got me inducted into the Glen Ridge High School Athletic Hall of Fame in the spring of 2016 by my high school guidance counselor and assistant track coach, Bill Indek. The induction ceremony was delayed until 2017 because a very deranged classmate thought they were worthier of the accolade than me and threatened in retaliation to "blow the place up like fireworks." In May 2017, with heavy police presence, my sister Jo had the honor of presenting my award. She was able to summarize my years of running into a matter of minutes, and provided the *Cliff Notes* for this book when she said:

Congratulations to all the honorees for your outstanding accomplishments. Your commitment to the world of athletics is truly remarkable.

I asked Sally to send me some information about her running career. Sally was kind enough to send me ten pages of information which started off when she was seven. Who keeps track of this stuff when they're seven? The answer? A serious, dedicated runner.

I'm going to fast-forward to her high school career. While at Glen Ridge High School, Sally became an outstanding runner competing in cross-country and winter and spring track all four years, not only earning twelve varsity letters but placing in every state meet in every season. Sally literally ran the extra mile. While her teammates and competitors were fast asleep, Sally woke up early, laced up her running shoes, and ran three miles down Ridgewood Avenue before school. She was rewarded by her hard work and diligence with running a personal record of 18:59 in her junior cross-country season, and this record stood for twenty-five years. She ran a 5:12 in the 1,500-meter run in her senior spring track season, and that record was broken thirteen years later. Her leadership skills were apparent at this early age as she was selected as captain for winter track in her senior year.

But being eligible for this fine honor is probably not just based on a high school career. As Springsteen likes to call them, Sally's "Glory Days" continued at Glassboro State College. Her perseverance as a four-year cross-country and track collegiate athlete earned Sally the position of captain for both cross-country and track teams in her junior and senior years. She improved her 1,500-meter time to an impressive 5:01. At Glassboro, not only did Sally accumulate medals, but also forged lifelong friendships with her teammates and roommates: Pam, SueAnn, and Linda.

After college, Sally continued to challenge her athletic abilities by competing in everything from 400 meters to marathons with some javelin and shot put thrown in for good measure. My sister Pat often acted as her training partner and shared with me some of Sally's unique training and racing strategies to help her attain her goals. Sometimes Sally would make up little songs, and at other times during a particularly grueling workout, she would pretend there was a magical rope pulling her toward the finish line. She has been an active member as both a competitor and volunteer in both the Ocean Running Club and the Jersey Shore Running Club where she won numerous awards.

Sally is probably most famous for developing the Pine Beach 5K. A few us know it as "The Sallaganza." This is a race that Sally founded and directed for over ten years and built up to a USATF-NJ Masters Championship Race with over 1,600 participants. The success of this race resulted in raising substantial funds which were distributed to Ocean County student scholarships, the Pine Beach Fire Department, First Aid Squad, and the Police Alcohol and Drug Awareness Program.

Everyone has heard the saying that you must learn to love yourself before you can love others. Well, Sally really excels at loving herself, as evident by the picture. Lest you think she is a narcissist, Sally has so much love in her that it literally bursts out of her in the form of generosity of time, money, and fun. Her passion for life is inclusive and contagious, whether she is inviting others to participate in the tower run ups, coaching her team of co-workers in their first 5K, or sometimes just inviting others to enjoy the simple pleasure of kayaking.

Sally is beautiful, talented, and surrounded by many loving friends and family, including her own three scholar athletes, Paula, Sam, and Dana. Like all of us, she has had her trials and tribulations, yet she embodies the Chinese proverb "Fall down seven times, get up eight." A few years back, while her husband was declining due to his cancer, she herself was diagnosed with multiple myeloma. This was a very trying time, but Sally prevailed and channeled her energy into stair climbing for charity. Over the past five years, between the Pine Beach 5K and the tower runs, Sally has raised over $110,000 for charity—all the while rising in the rankings for the tower runs to fifth in the United States and twentieth overall in the world.

One of her biggest challenges by far presented itself this past year. Sally's health needed attention due to the resurgence of multiple myeloma. This resulted in more than four weeks in the hospital and almost a year of chemotherapy. Her resiliency and tenacious spirit powered her through this difficult time. Now she is back and getting ready to participate in the invitation-only Eiffel Tower Run Up next March in Paris. And so Sally will continue her pursuit of more athletic endeavors.

I would like to thank the fine people of this athletic association for recognizing Sally Cavallaro Kalksma. You have chosen a very worthy person to add to the wonderful legacy of Glen Ridge High School.

Did you catch the part in her speech when she said, "Sally really excels at loving herself as evident by the picture"? Jo had a 22" x 26" poster of me showing off my muscles while wearing a shirt that said "I Love Me." The induction ceremony felt more like a roast. Everyone, including me, got a good laugh. When I accepted my plaque and poster, I responded:

The photo Jo had blown up. Only a sister could get away with doing something like this.

Thank you, JoAnne. Hi all, and congratulations to my fellow inductees, past inductees, and possibly future inductees here tonight. I am very honored to be among you. I read up on your accomplishments, and they truly are amazing.

I want to thank Bill Indek and the committee for this induction. Hey, committee, I bet you didn't realize all the drama that would come with inducting someone from the class of 1980. Sorry about that. Seriously, thank God Frank Gerard is the only one here from my class tonight.

I do wish our cross-country coach, Scott Mein, was here so I could apologize to him for being such a brat. And that is a mild word—I gave him such a hard time. I was so difficult to coach. But Coach Mein can thank me because I probably got him a spot in heaven right alongside four other people who unfortunately are no longer here: Our track coach and class advisor, Craig Lawrence—what a great man; my father, the infamous and very tough Coach Sam Cavallaro; my mother, my biggest fan till the day she died—she was at every race, rain or shine, cheering and yelling, "Run like hell"; and my late husband. Although I didn't meet Pete until I was a freshman in college, he supported and pushed me to continue running when I was burnt out. When we met, I told him I wasn't going to go out for track, and he said, "What are you going to do? Get fat like the rest of the chicks in college?" I'm so glad he said that because I wouldn't have met my three best friends, one of whom is here: Linda Schlachter.

To this day we all still train and compete together. But most of all we have fun, and that is what sports should be about. Although my husband is not here, his spirit lives on in my three beautiful, smart, and athletic children: Paula, Sam, and Dana. My daughters are here tonight, and I'm happy to say they now run with me. Nothing is greater than having your children share your sport with you.

So, there are four people who are here tonight that I have to thank. They are the reason I started to run. In fact, they are the reason why I have done anything good in my life. I have always looked up to and admired them, and I wanted to be just like them. They are my four sisters: Marion, JoAnne, Pat, and Sue. In fact, my first long run was with Marion when we ran from our house in Point to the baby beach. And Jo, Pat, and Sue were instrumental in founding the girls track and cross-country teams at GR. However, there is one sister I have to point out. Not that I am playing favorites, because we all know in my family, I am the only favorite. When I qualified for the Meet of Champs my freshman year, I called Pat at college, and she said, "Oh, you're gonna get killed. I gotta come home and help you." And she did, for the next four years and beyond. We ran twice a day—in the mornings down Ridgewood Ave, and in the afternoons, endless quarters around that crazy round cinder track. She became my mentor, my inspiration, my nemesis, and my rival—since we both ran the same event, the mile. But it made us better athletes and competitors, and we formed a special bond. And that is what sports does. So, thank you, Pat, and all my sisters. You are the best sisters in the whole world. And I love you all so much.

While I'm on the topic of family and induction ceremonies, here is an old photograph of my sisters and me at a dedication ceremony for a weight room named in honor of my father. From left: the twins, Sue and Pat, Marion, Jo, and me.

TRAINING LOG
DATE: May 28, 2017
EVENT: Race Day – Spring Lake 5 Mile Run
TIME: Ran/walked with Jo, Pam, and Linda in 1:11.
NOTES: Felt great! Had fun!

If you stop doing what you love, then the cancer has won. I love running, whether it's vertical or horizontal, and I was not going to let cancer win. Fifteen weeks after my SCT, I hit my goal: five miles. But I wasn't done. Since there were no stair climb races until the fall, I signed up for the Pine Beach 5K, which was a month later. My goal was to run the entire thing without walking. I hit that goal, too, thanks to Paula pushing me the entire 3.1 miles. Next on my list was my first stair climb that September: the Bennington Monument in Vermont. I choose this race for several reasons: 1) it was very important to me to keep challenging myself; 2) it was the first stair climb on the schedule; 3) I had never done it before so I couldn't compare myself to my past; 4) I had the option to climb the monument one or two times; and 5) it was one of the shortest climbs in the country at just 412 steps to the top, which was good since I was not yet healed from the Liz Franc fracture in my left foot. Despite the pain, it was great to be back racing. My nephew Rob, who lived close by, joined me and my teammates, the Tower Masters. We all chose the option to climb up the battlefield monument twice for a total of 824 steps. Stair climbing was about to take a larger box in my life again.

That summer I started back on the chemo. I would have to continue taking the Revlimad every night for an undetermined amount of time to keep the multiple myeloma cells suppressed and my numbers in the normal range. I told myself that everyone gets some ailment when they get older, and I got multiple myeloma. Most people end up on some type of medication, too, be it for heart, diabetes, blood pressure, or whatever. I was on chemo. The side effects of Revlimad became my new normal. I also was still dealing with the long-term side effects of the SCT, which included cramps, weakness, and joint swelling. One side effect that I never thought too much about until it gave me a scare was the possibility of a false reading of normal cells. During my annual gynecological exam, the gynecologist found abnormal cells. Over the course of the next three months, the doctor performed several other procedures before determining that I needed surgery to remove an area that showed cervical cancer. Yes, I was silently freaking out, as I didn't want to put my family through any more hardship. Dr. S assured me and the gynecologist that I did not need surgery and that my cells would return to normal within a year. Dr. S was right. My cells returned to normal. I did not have cervical cancer.

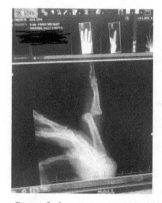

One of the many injuries I succumbed to, thanks to the neuropathy.

Unfortunately, neuropathy was not one of the side effects that was getting better. I was constantly working around injuries. But it was okay—I was alive! I practiced the grit I knew so well and learned to manage the neuropathy. This grit was admired by the HEADstrong Foundation. They called to tell me I was the recipient of the Nicholas Colleluori Award for a survivor demonstrating heroic perseverance in the fight against cancer. At the black-tie banquet in Philadelphia, I had the opportunity to speak in front of hundreds in attendance. I told them about my memories of reading about Nick Colleluori while I was in treatment at UPenn. I had been doing laps around the hall when a picture of a young man caught my eye. His story hit home. He was just a freshman in college when he was diagnosed with cancer. I remembered meeting his mother when they served me and the other patients ice cream on Valentine's Day. I felt honored to be recognized, as I felt that I was a part of the HEADstrong family. The next day I flew to Paris to participate in my long anticipated La Tour de Eiffel.

The MMRF, along with the pharmaceutical company, Amgen (the maker of Neupogen, the drug I had to administer to myself prior to my SCT), sponsored my 2018 racing season, which included my race in

Accepting the Nicholas Colleluori Award from the HEADstrong Foundation.

France. I was now appearing on television stations all over the world. When I reached the top of the Eiffel Tower, I looked down and thought about how far I had come in a year. Twelve months ago I could barely walk. At that moment, on the top of the Iron Lady, I realized that my story could go beyond athletics and change lives. I realized I wanted to help and inspire others. It was my "aha," eureka moment.

My friends at the MMRF have always called me their "media darling." For the past six years I helped promote the MMRF on TV and radio. They arranged for me to appear on such shows as *The Today Show with Natalie Morales, World News Tonight,* and *Channel 7 Eyewitness News* with my dear friend and meteorologist Amy Freeze. Amy, too, has brought much-needed awareness to the MMRF and helped us promote and raise funds. I was never camera shy—I had my television debut in college when I appeared in a 1980s music video wearing practically nothing but paint for a Philadelphia-based rock band. Later I did several local TV and radio spots promoting the Pine Beach 5K.

When I returned to the States, I had interviews lined up before and after every race. It seemed that everyone wanted to share my story. I appeared on the *Preston and Steve Show* and *Fox News,* and there was a large write-up in the *Philadelphia Inquirer.* I even had the honor, along with a few other MMRF teammates, of ringing the opening bell at the New York Stock Exchange. These public appearances led me to start doing motivational speaking. I loved giving hope to those who think they can't do something because of their diagnosis. In the midst of all of these appearances, an acquaintance said to me, "Cancer is the best thing that ever happened to you." I abruptly replied, "No, it's not, but I made the best of it."

Not everyone liked my public appearances. In fact, some people tried, but did not succeed, to knock me down. I did not stoop to their level when they bashed me for appearing in a political commercial. To me, the commercial was about supporting the person I believed was the most qualified for the job as a senator. The commercial wasn't about me, yet I found myself needing to defend myself and my past. Yes, I lent a friend money. I would lend someone the shirt off my back—well, as long as I was wearing a decent bra, I would. And that is exactly the attitude I had when the good cops-bad cops from the Intelligence Section of the New Jersey State Police showed up at my door to question me. Their roles were right out of a movie. Bad cop Detective David was a tall, well-built, good-looking former Division 1 linebacker who didn't say a word. I think I was supposed to be intimidated by his presence. Detective Pat was the good cop, a short, pleasant, middle-aged man. I couldn't help but make jokes to them as they sat at my kitchen table. Bad cop didn't think I was funny. Good cop laughed. However, it was no joke when I was subpoenaed to appear in court, where I told the truth, the whole truth, and nothing but the truth, so help me God. Although I lack faith in God, I do have in faith in people. I don't care what religion they are, what they believe in, or if they pray to Jesus,

It's very important to find what makes you happy. Here I am all smiles aboard my "lifeboat." MY BuOy TOY came along and literally rescued me when I needed something positive in my life. Photo by Tom Zapcic Photography.

Buddha, or a sphinx, as long as they follow the Ten Commandments, just as I do. It's that simple. Wouldn't this world be such a better place if everyone was a little kinder? We have natural disasters that put us in peril. We don't need the human race to do that too.

TRAINING LOG
DATE: December 18, 2018
WORKOUT: Lunch – Stairs, 50 floors; Night – 48 minutes of hills
NOTES: Felt good/strong

It was time for a new challenge. I hit all my goals in 2018: I did eleven tower races and two road races. I knew I could run up any building twice, but could I run up fifty floors twelve times? Could I do the Dallas Vertical Mile before the two-and-a-half-hour cut-off? Not only would I have to have the speed to finish and the endurance to complete the 9,684 vertical steps, but I would have to strategically pace myself; in this tower race, they not only timed the ascent, but they also included the elevator ride back down in the allotted time to finish. That gave me less than thirteen minutes for each round trip up and down the Reunion Tower in Dallas. And could I do all this while still on Revlimad? YES! I did not want to cut it close in case I cramped up, so I paced myself at eight-and-a-half minutes for each round trip. I completed the race with thirty minutes to spare and a time of one hour and forty-five minutes. Celgene, the maker of Revlimad, was quite impressed. Joel Beetsch, the VP of Patient Advocacy at Celgene, asked me to be a patient advocate. I was bestowed this honor at a dinner with Mark Alles, the CEO of Celgene, and Giovanni Caforio, the CEO of Bristol-Meyers Squibb. I was thrilled that I could reach out and help more people. My aha moment from a year earlier was becoming a reality. My momentum toward my new goal in life was in full swing.

When meeting new people, I always listen to what they have to say and ask as many questions as I can get in. The 2019 ESBRU was no different when marathon great Meb Keflezighi was the MMRF ambassador. I had the pleasure of spending the day with him prior to the race. We had lunch and did a photo shoot. I knew this was a once-in-a-lifetime opportunity to ask one of the best distance runners of all times for some racing tips. He told me that as I get older, I would have to stretch more. I have always stretched, but now I stretch more. And you know what? I'm racing well, and injury-free!

TRAINING LOG
DATE: February 22, 2020
EVENT: Albany CF Climb
TIME: 42 floors – 8:15; 3rd overall female

My 2020 stair climbing season started out great. I was finally free from injuries and training well. This was evident when I competed in my first race of the season and cut nine seconds off my time from the previous year. In 2019, I was the sixth overall female finisher. This year I was the third overall female to reach top of the Corning Tower in New York. A week later I had another podium finish when I once again took third overall at the Fight for Air Stair Climb in Baltimore, Maryland. Not only did I have a good "race" time, I had a great time "at" the race. My son-in-law Rob and my boyfriend, Jett, both participated in the event with Linda and me. I love encouraging people to try things outside of their comfort zone. In addition to getting Linda, Jett, my son-in-law Rob, my nephew Rob, Dana, and her boyfriend Derek to try stair climbing, I was even able to coax my sister Jo, her husband, Dennis, my niece Jackie, my cousin Keith, and my friend Van to try a stair climb race. Not everyone gets hooked on running up a zillion steps as fast as they can, but my hope is that, having had this experience with me, they may be inspired to keep challenging themselves to find what boosts their confidence and motivates them to make positive changes in their lives for their mental and physical health. It's all about finding what moves you.

There were another nine races left on my schedule when COVID-19 hit. The 2020 pandemic not only canceled the stair climb season, it shut down *everything*. Our way of life and our way of living changed indefinitely. Unfortunately, due to my low immune system, I was one of the unlucky ones who got Covid. But I didn't come this far to be taken down by the coronavirus. Improving my current fiftieth world ranking would have to wait since, once again, life gets in the way. However, a silver lining is that I don't need races to help me connect with and reach out to others dealing with cancer. As always, I shifted all the boxes in my life. I started a Facebook page called "No Wigs Needed," which focuses on using laughter as medicine. This positive site is a place for cancer patients, family members, friends, and caregivers to proudly share their upbeat stories and post photos of their treatment, operations, and life with cancer, regardless of their hair status. I was inspired to launch this site when a good friend asked me to do the honor of shaving her head when she started to lose her hair due to her breast cancer treatment. We laughed together during her brave ordeal. I also started blogging on my website, sallykalksma.com, posted articles in the New York Cancer Resource Alliance (NYCRA), and had virtual media interviews on radio stations, including iHeartRadio with fitness guru Tom Holland. NYCRA then asked me to host a video talk show that highlights new innovations in the healthcare field. I became an "Honored Hero" for the Leukemia Lymphoma Society and a "Move for Myeloma Ambassador" for the MMRF.

This is not the end. Each day is a new beginning. I plan on doing a lot more because I have the ability to try something new—or start all over again. I don't plan on going anywhere anytime soon, but when I finally do go, you better believe that if I go to hell, I'm going to spread some hope. And if there is a heaven, and Saint Peter lets me in, then watch out, because I'm going to cause a whole lot of ruckus up there. But for now, I'm here to stay. I had multiple myeloma. It didn't have me.

EPILOGUE

Life got in the way, and it brought me so many great experiences with all of its twists and turns. I am extremely lucky to have had the ability to push my body beyond its limit by competing in over seventy international tower races thus far. I am very grateful that I have had the opportunity to use my athletic ability to touch so many lives in a positive way, making over thirty public appearances worldwide to date. I have and will continue to proudly support the Multiple Myeloma Research Foundation, the International Myeloma Foundation, the Leukemia Lymphoma Society, Damon Cancer Research, Multiple Scoliosis, Cystic Fibrosis, The Stephen Siller Foundation, Her Justice, Special Olympics, American Lung Association, World Wildlife Foundation, HEADstrong Foundation, the Rehabilitation Institute of Chicago, and the Challenged Athletes Foundation.

If there is anything you take away from reading this book, I hope it's that you realize you have the power to make a positive change in your life, as well as in the lives of others. You can train your brain, dig deep for some grit, keep the grace, and make your life better by rearranging some boxes. And don't forget to have some fun along the way!

"Sally's Rubik's Cube" by Theo Rindos

ACKNOWLEDGMENTS

This book wouldn't have been possible without all those who have touched my life in some way, positive or negative. However, there are several people that need to be recognized for putting up with me, and they are my children: Paula, Sam, and Dana—my moral compass. You three continuously point me in the right direction with your strength, intelligence, and bravery. I have to admit that each of you have become "the smartest in the house" with your post-graduate degrees from the University of Delaware, Columbia University, and New York Law School.

I also want to thank Jett Simon for teaching me how to slow down and match my socks. Some people can never find the right person. I was lucky enough to find the right person a second time in my life when he realized I wasn't a "bitch"—I just couldn't dock my new boat.

A team of seven women were "literally" responsible for this book: my editor, Claudia Volkman, who has the patience of a saint (I'm sorry this book took me so long to write, but life gets in the way); my marketer and mentor, Lauren Georgiades, who has wisdom beyond her years and is the perfect combination of goofiness and professionalism; my "stepsister" and author of *See Jane Climb*, Jane Trahanovsky, who helped me take the "first step" in writing this book and, like a true teammate, encouraged me to the finish; my publisher, Karen Strauss, and her assistant, Sara Foley, who both mentored and guided me in uncharted territory; my graphic designer, Natasha Clawson, whose beautiful work doesn't even compare to the beauty she possesses, inside and out; and Jane Hoffman, who has always been there for me, like family, along with the entire Multiple Myeloma Research Foundation.

My sincerest gratitude to all those who were there for me when I was going through treatment, and to those who supported me when I was healthy and racing up tall buildings. I appreciate those who were there when I was both sick and running up the stairs at the same time. Your encouragement has inspired me to be a better person.

Please note: If you do not see your name, it does not mean you were not a muse. It means the book had to be edited.

I wish I had a dollar for every hour I've spent in a waiting room. I could have used all that money to help find a cure for cancer. Instead, I channeled this dream into raising money for cancer research by racing up tall buildings. I've also pledged a portion of the sales of this book to the Multiple Myeloma Research Foundation. Thank you, not only for purchasing my book, but for helping those living with multiple myeloma.

Thank you all for reading this book.

RECIPES

I'm Italian; I love to eat. To me, food is sacred. I'm not going to pretend I'm a chef. I can read; therefore, I can cook. This is not a cookbook. However, I do have a few signature dishes that seem to impress people. I can't take credit for coming up with all of them, just for tweaking them to perfection. I also believe that you only live once, and yes, you should live a healthy lifestyle. Food is fuel for your body, and you should put the best fuel in it so it performs well, but you shouldn't deny yourself the pleasure of a good meal or a good drink, especially when going thorough cancer treatment. "Comfort food" makes you feel good.

Nonna's Meatballs

I wish I had my grandmother's recipe, but this one is probably just as good.

In a large bowl mix together:

2 lbs of ground beef/pork/veal
2 eggs
1 cup of Cento Italian breadcrumbs
½ cup of parmesan cheese
¼ cup of fresh chopped parsley
2 tsp salt
1 tsp pepper
1 tsp garlic powder

Roll into small balls, and cook, turning often, in a pan of olive oil on the stove.

Josephine's Gravy

My sister, Jo, was named after my grandmother Guisepa, or in America, Josephine. So, it's no wonder she is a great cook. Here is a recipe that is so easy you should never have to buy a jar of gravy again:

Sauté an onion, one bay leaf, and garlic in olive oil.
Throw in one 28-oz can of tomato sauce, one 8-oz can of tomato paste, and a stick of butter.
Add salt, pepper, and optional Italian seasoning or hot pepper flakes. DONE!
If adding meatballs, let them simmer in the gravy for an hour. You can sauté any leftover veggies in olive oil and add them to your gravy too. Just remember to remove the onion and bay leaf before serving.

Moist Turkey

This is what turkey is supposed to taste like!

Note: The size of the turkey will determine how long you cook it for. Be sure to have a pop-up timer in the bird, and a cooking thermostat to check the internal temperature.

Defrost bird in fridge.

Preheat oven to 350 degrees.

Rinse thoroughly inside and out.

Salt all sides and inside.

(You can add stuffing for more flavor or to make it moister, but I don't.)

Put backside up on a rack in a roasting pan with a couple of inches of water on the bottom. (Do not let the water touch the turkey.)

Cut up an onion and put it around the turkey in the water.

Cover completely with a cheesecloth that has been presoaked in three sticks of melted margarine

Baste EVERY 30 minutes.

Halfway through, take the cheesecloth off, turn the turkey over, and put the cheesecloth back on.

Continue basting every 30 minutes.

The last hour, take the cheesecloth off and continue to baste every half hour.

Turn the turkey over again for the last half hour to brown the other side too.

While waiting for the turkey to cool before slicing, you can make the gravy:

Take the water from the roasting pan, add, salt, pepper, flour, and Gravy Master to taste.

Heat in a pot on the stove.

Sweet Potato Soup

This annual Thanksgiving tradition is hearty enough as a meal anytime of the year.

Put 2 tablespoons of butter in a pan on the stove and cook the following vegetables until tender:
    4 sliced carrots
    4 sliced celery stalks
    2 large onions cut up
    2 bay leaves

In a large pot combine:
    80 oz of vegetable stock
    1 cup of water
    I cup of white wine
    3 pounds of peeled, cubed sweet potatoes
    1 lb of peeled cubed white potatoes

    Add vegetables from pan.
    Bring to a boil, then simmer uncovered for 40 minutes.
    Remove bay leaves and blend mixture until smooth.
    Return to pot and reheat adding a teaspoon each of salt, nutmeg, and white pepper.

Pat's Pizza Bread

My sister Pat has perfected Pepperoni Bread. No matter how hard I try, mine never tastes as good as hers. She said an electric oven cooks better than gas (but a gas stove top is better than electric). Go figure. She even plays around with this recipe by filling it with different vegetables. I never had too much luck when I tried it. Here's the original:

Bread:
    1 cup of milk
    2/3 stick of butter
    3 T of sugar
    1 tsp of salt
    3 cups of flour
    1 package of active dry yeast
    ½ cup of warm water

Filling:
    1 stick of pepperoni, cut in ¼ inch cubes
    One 3 oz package of mozzarella cheese, also cut in ¼-inch cubes

To cook:
Stir milk, butter, sugar and salt over medium heat until it boils. Remove from stove and let stand until warm. In a large bowl dissolve yeast in warm water. Stir in milk mixture. Add flour, one cup at a time. Mix until dough is easy to handle. Cover and let rise in warm place until it doubles, about one to two hours. Punch dough (my favorite part)!

Spread dough into a rectangle on a lightly greased cookie sheet. Spread the pepperoni and mozzarella down the center of the dough. Fold one side of the dough and then the other side over the top. Fold ends under the loaf. Make sure none of the filling is peeking out. Bake at 400 degrees for 25–35 minutes or until golden brown. Immediately remove the bread from the cookie sheet and place on a cutting board. This tastes best when it is served warm.

Smilin' Sal's Homemade Limoncello

You can drink this delicious beverage as a shot, sip it after a meal, add to club soda with ice as a cocktail, or pour over vanilla ice cream as an intoxicating tasty dessert. You can also substitute other citrus fruits for the lemons. I've tried making it with oranges, and it was delicious too.

Take the rinds only, do not peel, from 20 organic rinsed lemons (or any citrus fruit)
Put in a large pot with 1.75 liters of 190 proof Everclear
Cover and let sit for 14-21 days in the dark at room temperature
When the rinds turn brittle and white they are done
Filter the alcohol from the rinds
In a large pot bring 12 cups of water to a boil and slowly stir in 10 lbs of sugar
Stir constantly
Turn off and let the simple syrup come to room temperature.
When totally cool, add it to the alcohol and mix well.
Fill twelve 750-ml bottles
Let sit in a cool dark place for a minimum of forty-five days.

Special Recipe

Here is another recipe that calls for lemons: lemon water. Yes, that's it. Fill a glass of water, add ice and squeeze some lemon. Not only does this quench your thirst, but it helps remove toxins from your body and fills up your stomach so you don't eat as much. Plus, the flavor makes it easier to consume the obligatory eight glasses a day. Growing up in the '70s, we never had water breaks. It had to be a minimum of 110 degrees with a matching humidity for me to drink out of the gum-infested water fountain during track and cross country practice. It wasn't until I met Linda at college that she made me her "special recipe." She filled up a glass with water and ice, and handed it to me after a tough night of drinking—it was *sooo* good!

Desserts

There is no recipe here—just some advice. Are you really hungry when dessert is served after a big meal? I'm not. If I am still hungry, then I need to put better fuel in my body. Not desserts. However, if I just want the taste of something sweet, I allow myself to give into temptation, especially chocolate—BUT I just take a sliver or small piece to get the taste. That's all I need to satisfy my taste buds.

WORKOUTS

Just as I'm not a doctor, I'm not a certified coach either. However, I know a lot since I've run around the block quite a bit during my fifty-plus years of exercising. Therefore, I will share with you some basic workouts that help maintain your body like a well-oiled machine. Be sure to always change up your workouts to shake up your muscles. Now I'll add the obligatory medical disclaimer and tell you to consult with a doctor before trying any strenuous activities—although I never do. I usually tell my oncologist afterward, and he just shakes his head.

How to Start Running

Just run; it's that basic. The more you run, the faster you will get. A human is an animal. You, the human, are designed to run. If you haven't run since you were a child, then start with baby steps again. No, not tiny steps—just start at the beginning again. Walk a block, then run to the nearest mailbox, walk another block, then try running again to the next mailbox, or whatever landmark you are comfortable with. Eventually you will run longer and walk shorter until one day you are no longer walking. There, that's all there is to learning how to run again. Don't worry about your form, or your time. Just run.

I love to watch children run. They just go outside and play all day. They don't know to take a break and rest. They don't know to stop and drink water. They just run around until they are tired. No one says, "Rest one minute, and do that all over again, then repeat five times." I've always enjoyed watching children run their first race. I call it "Running Stupid." The children are not yet coached. They just run with all their heart. Yes, some children hit the wall and die halfway through the race, but some just go. They go as fast as they can until they finish. They don't know any better. As we get older, we are told what to do and how to do it. Sure, some of it is for the best. But some of it can take the pure enjoyment out of it.

Let's face it, running isn't really that fun. The high you get when you finish is. So why take what little fun there is in running and ruin it? Just go out and run. Don't say you CAN'T do it. Remember what I wrote earlier in the book about staying positive and not using negative words. If you say you can't do it, then your body will stop. If you say you can, then your body will go. Do you think a caveman said, "I can't run," when a Tyrannosaurus Rex was chasing him? Look who's extinct now!

Fartlek

This does not mean running as fast as you can to the nearest bathroom. *Fartlek* is a Swedish word for "speed play." When you fartlek, you run at various speeds, usually a very fast pace, followed by a slower recovery run, and you keep repeating this, with no exact pace or distance. Unlike a speed workout on the track, fartleking is usually done on the road, hills, or trails. Some other misleading terms in running are LSD and speed. When a runner says they are doing LSD, and then the next day you hear they're doing speed, do not be alarmed. They are not doing drugs. LSD stands for Long Slow Distance, the backbone of training. Runners must build up a base to enable them to do other workouts, which include speed: a fast, intense workout.

Lifting

Perfect form is a must when it comes to lifting weights. If you're new to using weights, then make sure you have someone show you exactly how to do a specific exercise. You can always find something on YouTube; just make sure the instructor is a certified trainer with good credentials. Fitness expert Tom Holland has a lot of great videos.

I'm very old fashioned when it comes to weight training. Sometimes I like good, old-fashioned calisthenics (push-ups, sits-ups, leg raisers, etc.) that use my own body weight, much like Jack LaLanne did. Other times I use dumbbells. When I use free weights, I constantly change my workout each time to keep my muscles fresh. One day I may do three sets of twelve to fifteen reps at a heavy weight. Another day, I may do one set to failure (as many as I can) with a lighter weight. Often I go from one set to another with little or no rest. I love to constantly mix things up. I follow @taychayy on Instagram. Trainer Taylor Chamberlain Dilk constantly changes up her intense workouts.

Stair Climbing, also called Tower Running

Running up the stairs is very difficult, but with the proper technique it is doable. Before I get into exactly how to run up the stairs, I need to explain the difference between flights and floors. A floor, which is also called a story, is made up of one or more flights. A flight of stairs is a staircase going up in one direction. A flight ends when it hits a landing. The next flight starts when you make the turn on that landing. If you are running in a building, a floor or story will usually have a door on each floor. Towers are usually structures with no floors. Buildings with high ceilings have more flights to each floor, or story, therefore more stairs. No two buildings are alike. Older buildings usually have steep, narrow stairwells. Newer buildings have a wider stairwell with steps that are not as steep because they are built to certain codes. Either way, you always take at least two steps at a time! No excuses.

Keep your body slightly bent at an angle so you're not fighting gravity too much, but keep your head up, as not to restrict your airflow. Make sure you keep your eyes down so you don't trip, which usually happens as you start to feel fatigued and have difficulty lifting your legs. The width of the staircase is important when climbing stairs as there are two ways to go about it:

1. If the stairwell is narrow, you can grab each handrail on either side and pull yourself up as you run up the stairs. You can also use an alternate arm motion, like cross-country skiing. It is very important to use your upper body when climbing.
2. If the stairwell is too wide to grab each handrail, use the handrail on the inner side, and pull yourself up with a hand-over-hand motion, much like climbing a rope. When using either form, make sure to take full advantage of the upcoming landing by grabbing the handrail on the next flight and propelling your body around like a slingshot.

There is one more super-duper important tip: never, ever look at what floor number you're on. This can instantly psych you out when you realize you are nowhere near the top. You don't want to make stair climbing any harder than it already is. When finished, be sure to always take the elevator down to avoid the impact of your body weight on your joints.

Quarters

NO, NOT THE DRINKING GAME! Just as doing LSD and Speed does not mean drugs in running, Quarters does not mean drinking. Quarters means one lap around a running track. Four quarters on a regulation track equals a mile. Regulation tracks are either 400 meters or 440 yards. Quarters are the staple in any running workout. How do you do a quarter? The same way you run, just faster. My favorite speed workout consists of a mile warm-up in the opposite direction on the track. You need to balance your body. Years of running in the same direction will cause an uneven gait and possible injuries. I then do ten quarters at a specific pace. I then do a mile cooldown, again in the opposite direction.

Hills

My favorite running work out is "Hills." The concept is easy; the workout is hard. Run up a hill as fast as you can, and slowly go down to recover. Repeat this several times, depending on the length of the hill and how many miles you're doing. As in all hard workouts, run a warm-up and do a cooldown after. I do this on a flat surface.

Stretching

If you don't take my advice, then take it from Meb Keflezighi. This professional marathoner won both the New York City Marathon and the Boston Marathon, as well as placed second in the Olympics. He told me to stretch MORE. Notice he said "more." You should always stretch to prevent injuries. Proper form is a must to maximize the benefits of stretching. If you aren't sure what to do, watch a YouTube video. *Yoga with Adrienne* is one of my faves. I like gentle stretch yoga moves after a hard workout.

THE SKYSCRAPERS I HAVE CLIMBED IN SALLY WORLD

During my fifty-plus years of running, I have competed in everything from a fifty-yard dash to a marathon, including throwing a javelin to completing a triathlon, and just about everything else in between. My favorite event by far is stair climbing. Nothing is more challenging than running vertically, and nothing is more rewarding than being on top of the world when you look down from the top of a tower, knowing you gave it your all to get there.

I love to step on the starting line in the lobby on the first floor and turn on the switch in my head. I want the best for any friends, family, and teammates in the race, but they will temporarily turn into my enemy, my competition, my nemesis until I finish. I have one goal: to do the best I can no matter what it takes.

Here is a list of some of the structures I have raced up. Some of them I ran up multiple times in one day, and others I have run up and then crossed town and ran up another. Some have even started in the basement to add an extra floor, while others have added some running at the top. While most have floors, some of these are only constructed with steps. I try to race up almost all of these buildings annually.

The CN Tower, Toronto, Canada – 1815 feet, 1776 steps

The Willis Tower (formerly The Sears Tower), Chicago, IL – 1354 feet, 103 floors

The Freedom Tower at One World Trade Center, New York, NY – 1268 feet, 105 floors

The Empire State Building, New York, NY – 1250 feet, 86 floors

The Stratosphere, Las Vegas, NV – 1149 feet, 1455 steps

The Eiffel Tower, Paris, France – 1063 feet, 1665 steps

4 World Trade Center, New York, NY – 977 feet, 72 floors

Rockefeller Center, New York, NY – 872 feet, 66 floors

BNY Mellon Building, Philadelphia, PA – 792 feet, 53 floors

300 North LaSalle, Chicago, IL – 784 feet, 60 floors

One Penn Plaza, New York, NY – 751 feet, 57 floors

The Viacom Building, New York, NY – 745 feet, 54 floors

Three Logan Square, Philadelphia, PA – 739 feet, 50 floors

FMC Tower, Philadelphia, PA – 730 feet, 47 floors

One Boston Place, Boston, MA – 601 feet, 41 floors

Corning Tower, Albany, NY – 589 feet, 42 floors

32 Old Slip at One Financial Square, New York, NY – 575 feet, 36 floors

The Helmsley Building, New York, NY – 565 feet, 35 floors

The Reunion Tower, Dallas, TX – 561 feet, 50 floors

The Skyscrapers I Have Climbed in Sally World

100 East Pratt, Baltimore, MD – 385 feet, 27 floors

The Chase Manhattan Centre, Wilmington, DE – 360 feet, 23 floors

One Gateway Center - Newark, NJ – 359 feet, 27 floors

The Bennington Monument, Bennington, VT – 306 feet, 417 steps

CPSIA information can be obtained
at www.ICGtesting.com
Printed in the USA
LVHW031039211220
674731LV00005B/424